D1497416

CONTENTS

ACT I

Scene I - P.005 Scene II - P.026
Scene III - P.057 Scene IV - P.070 Scene V - P.081

ACT II

Scene I - P.104 Scene II - P.115

ACT III

Scene I - P.185 Scene II - P.212
Scene III - P.261 Scene IV - P.270

ACT IV

Scene I - P.298 Scene II - P.303
Scene III - P.307 Scene IV - P.316 Scene V - P.323
Scene VI - P.349 Scene VII - P.353

ACT V

Scene I - P.371 Scene II - P.407

Bonus Materials - P.466

HOW TO READ MANGA!
Hello there, and welcome to Manga Classics! "Manga" is a style of comic book originating in Japan.
A manga book is read from right-to-left, which is backwards from the normal books you know. This means that you will find the first page where you expect to find the last page! It also means that each page begins in the top right corner.
START HERE!
1
2
3
4
5
6
7
Got the hang of it? Then you're ready to start reading Manga Classics!

ACT I
SCENE I
CHEE
CHEE
CHEE
ELSINORE.
A PLATFORM BEFORE
THE CASTLE.
STEP
CHEE
CHEE!

NAY, ANSWER ME: STAND, AND UNFOLD YOURSELF.
AH!
WHO'S THERE?
LONG LIVE THE KING!
SHUDDER
HE.
BERNARDO?
FRANCISCO
BERNARDO

YOU COME MOST CAREFULLY UPON YOUR HOUR.
'TIS NOW STRUCK TWELVE; GET THEE TO BED, FRANCISCO.

HAVE YOU HAD QUIET GUARD?

BRRR
FOR THIS RELIEF MUCH THANKS:
'TIS BITTER COLD, AND I AM SICK AT HEART.

WELL, GOOD NIGHT. IF YOU DO MEET HORATIO AND MARCELLUS, THE RIVALS OF MY WATCH, BID THEM MAKE HASTE.

NOT A MOUSE STIRRING.

STEP...
STEP...
STEP...

STEP...
STEP...

I THINK I HEAR THEM.

PHEW!
GIVE YOU GOOD NIGHT.
FRIENDS TO THIS GROUND.
AND LIEGEMEN TO THE DANE.
STEP
STEP
O, FAREWELL, HONEST SOLDIER: WHO HATH RELIEVED YOU?
MARCELLUS
BERNARDO HAS MY PLACE. GIVE YOU GOOD NIGHT.
HOLLA! BERNARDO!
SAY, WHAT, IS HORATIO THERE?
A PIECE OF HIM.
HORATIO

WHAT, HAS THIS THING APPEAR'D AGAIN TO-NIGHT?
I HAVE SEEN NOTHING.
WELCOME, HORATIO: WELCOME, GOOD MARCELLUS.
TAK
TAK
TAK
TAK
HORATIO SAYS 'TIS BUT OUR FANTASY, AND WILL NOT LET BELIEF TAKE HOLD OF HIM TOUCHING THIS DREADED SIGHT, TWICE SEEN OF US:
TUSH, TUSH, 'TWILL NOT APPEAR.
THEREFORE I HAVE ENTREATED HIM ALONG WITH US TO WATCH THE MINUTES OF THIS NIGHT; THAT IF AGAIN THIS APPARITION COME, HE MAY APPROVE OUR EYES AND SPEAK TO IT.

WELL, SIT WE DOWN, AND LET US HEAR BERNARDO SPEAK OF THIS.

SIT DOWN AWHILE; AND LET US ONCE AGAIN ASSAIL YOUR EARS, THAT ARE SO FORTIFIED AGAINST OUR STORY WHAT WE HAVE TWO NIGHTS SEEN.

LAST NIGHT OF ALL, WHEN YOND SAME STAR THAT'S WESTWARD FROM THE POLE HAD MADE HIS COURSE TO ILLUME THAT PART OF HEAVEN WHERE NOW IT BURNS, MARCELLUS AND MYSELF, THE BELL THEN BEATING ONE -

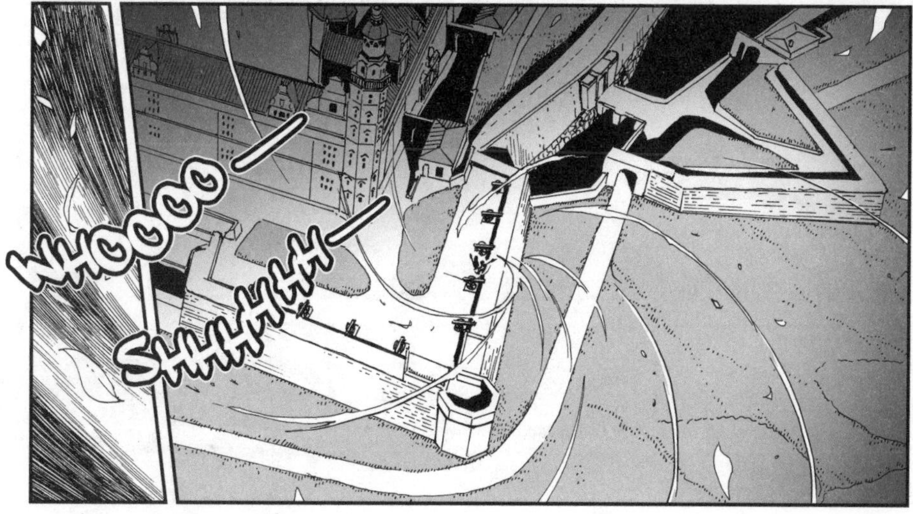
WHOOOO—
SHHHHH—

HHHAAAAAA~

!!

BRRR...
PEACE, BREAK THEE OFF; LOOK, WHERE IT COMES AGAIN!

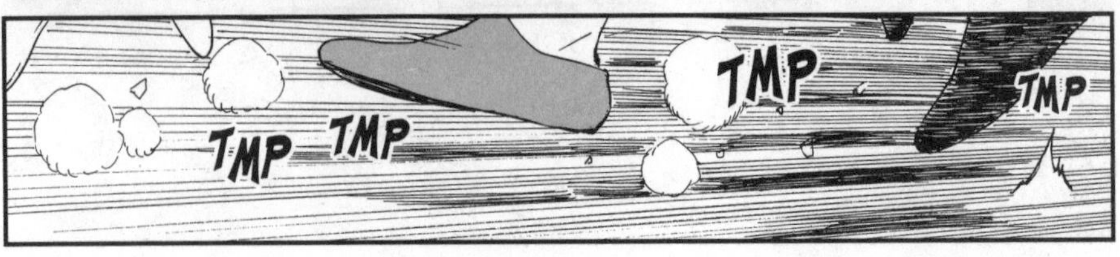

TMP
TMP
TMP
TMP

ZWIP!

HHHHHH...
IN THE SAME FIGURE, LIKE THE KING THAT'S DEAD.
THOU ART A SCHOLAR; SPEAK TO IT, HORATIO.
LOOKS IT NOT LIKE THE KING? MARK IT, HORATIO.

IT WOULD BE SPOKE TO.
MOST LIKE: IT HARROWS ME WITH FEAR AND WONDER.
SHOVE
QUESTION IT, HORATIO.
AH...

ooo
WHAT ART THOU THAT USURP'ST THIS TIME OF NIGHT, TOGETHER WITH THAT FAIR AND WARLIKE FORM IN WHICH THE MAJESTY OF BURIED DENMARK DID SOMETIMES MARCH?
BY HEAVEN I CHARGE THEE, SPEAK!

SEE, IT STALKS AWAY!

IT IS OFFENDED.

FUSSSSH—

STAY! SPEAK, SPEAK! I CHARGE THEE, SPEAK!
'TIS GONE, AND WILL NOT ANSWER.
!!
HOW NOW, HORATIO! YOU TREMBLE AND LOOK PALE:
IS NOT THIS SOMETHING MORE THAN FANTASY? WHAT THINK YOU ON'T?

BEFORE MY GOD, I MIGHT NOT THIS BELIEVE WITHOUT THE SENSIBLE AND TRUE AVOUCH OF MINE OWN EYES.
IS IT NOT LIKE THE KING?
AS THOU ART TO THYSELF: SUCH WAS THE VERY ARMOUR HE HAD ON WHEN HE THE AMBITIOUS NORWAY COMBATED;
SO FROWN'D HE ONCE, WHEN, IN AN ANGRY PARLE, HE SMOTE THE SLEDDED POLACKS ON THE ICE.
'TIS STRANGE.

THUS TWICE BEFORE, AND JUMP AT THIS DEAD HOUR, WITH MARTIAL STALK HATH HE GONE BY OUR WATCH.
IN WHAT PARTICULAR THOUGHT TO WORK I KNOW NOT;

BUT IN THE GROSS AND SCOPE OF MY OPINION, THIS BODES SOME STRANGE ERUPTION TO OUR STATE.

GOOD NOW, SIT DOWN,

AND TELL ME, HE THAT KNOWS, WHY THIS SAME STRICT AND MOST OBSERVANT WATCH SO NIGHTLY TOILS THE SUBJECT OF THE LAND,

AND WHY SUCH DAILY CAST OF BRAZEN CANNON, AND FOREIGN MART FOR IMPLEMENTS OF WAR;

HAAA...

WHY SUCH IMPRESS OF SHIPWRIGHTS, WHOSE SORE TASK DOES NOT DIVIDE THE SUNDAY FROM THE WEEK;

WHAT MIGHT BE TOWARD, THAT THIS SWEATY HASTE DOTH MAKE THE NIGHT JOINT-LABOURER WITH THE DAY: WHO IS'T THAT CAN INFORM ME?

THAT CAN I; AT LEAST, THE WHISPER GOES SO. OUR LAST KING, WHOSE IMAGE EVEN BUT NOW APPEAR'D TO US, WAS,

AS YOU KNOW, BY FORTINBRAS OF NORWAY, THERETO PRICK'D ON BY A MOST EMULATE PRIDE, DARED TO THE COMBAT; IN WHICH OUR VALIANT HAMLET - FOR SO THIS SIDE OF OUR KNOWN WORLD ESTEEM'D HIM - DID SLAY THIS FORTINBRAS; WHO BY A SEAL'D COMPACT,

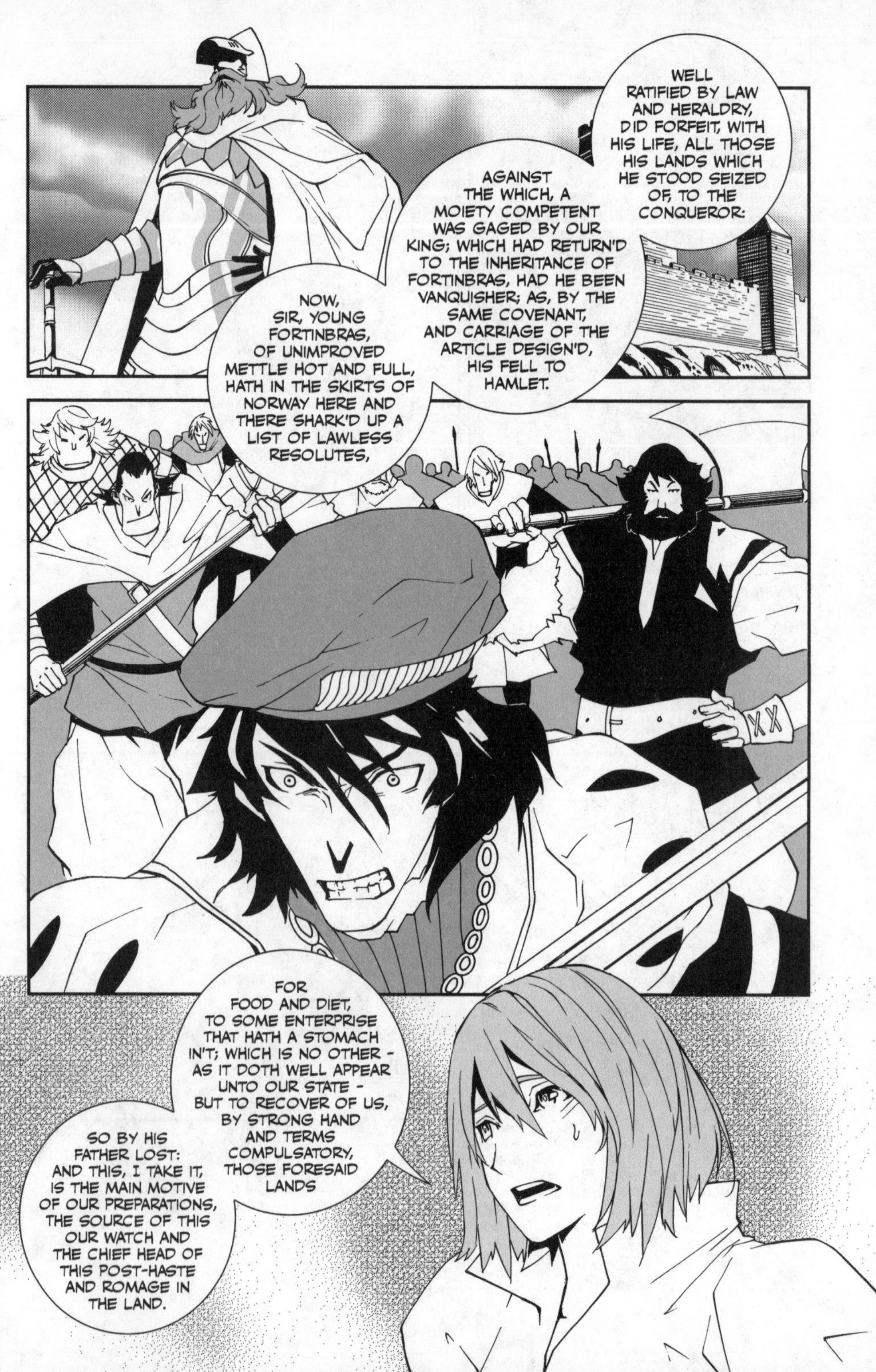
WELL RATIFIED BY LAW AND HERALDRY, DID FORFEIT, WITH HIS LIFE, ALL THOSE HIS LANDS WHICH HE STOOD SEIZED OF, TO THE CONQUEROR:
AGAINST THE WHICH, A MOIETY COMPETENT WAS GAGED BY OUR KING; WHICH HAD RETURN'D TO THE INHERITANCE OF FORTINBRAS, HAD HE BEEN VANQUISHER; AS, BY THE SAME COVENANT, AND CARRIAGE OF THE ARTICLE DESIGN'D, HIS FELL TO HAMLET.
NOW, SIR, YOUNG FORTINBRAS, OF UNIMPROVED METTLE HOT AND FULL, HATH IN THE SKIRTS OF NORWAY HERE AND THERE SHARK'D UP A LIST OF LAWLESS RESOLUTES,
FOR FOOD AND DIET, TO SOME ENTERPRISE THAT HATH A STOMACH IN'T; WHICH IS NO OTHER - AS IT DOTH WELL APPEAR UNTO OUR STATE - BUT TO RECOVER OF US, BY STRONG HAND AND TERMS COMPULSATORY, THOSE FORESAID LANDS
SO BY HIS FATHER LOST: AND THIS, I TAKE IT, IS THE MAIN MOTIVE OF OUR PREPARATIONS, THE SOURCE OF THIS OUR WATCH AND THE CHIEF HEAD OF THIS POST-HASTE AND ROMAGE IN THE LAND.

I THINK IT BE NO OTHER BUT E'EN SO: WELL MAY IT SORT THAT THIS PORTENTOUS FIGURE COMES ARMED THROUGH OUR WATCH; SO LIKE THE KING THAT WAS AND IS THE QUESTION OF THESE WARS.
A MOTE IT IS TO TROUBLE THE MIND'S EYE. IN THE MOST HIGH AND PALMY STATE OF ROME, A LITTLE ERE THE MIGHTIEST JULIUS FELL,
THE GRAVES STOOD TENANTLESS AND THE SHEETED DEAD DID SQUEAK AND GIBBER IN THE ROMAN STREETS: AS STARS WITH TRAINS OF FIRE AND DEWS OF BLOOD, DISASTERS IN THE SUN;
AND THE MOIST STAR UPON WHOSE INFLUENCE NEPTUNE'S EMPIRE STANDS WAS SICK ALMOST TO DOOMSDAY WITH ECLIPSE:
AND EVEN THE LIKE PRECURSE OF FIERCE EVENTS, AS HARBINGERS PRECEDING STILL THE FATES AND PROLOGUE TO THE OMEN COMING ON,
HAVE HEAVEN AND EARTH TOGETHER DEMONSTRATED UNTO OUR CLIMATURES AND COUNTRYMEN.

BUT SOFT, BEHOLD! LO, WHERE IT COMES AGAIN!
HHHHH

STAY, ILLUSION!
IF THOU HAST ANY SOUND, OR USE OF VOICE, SPEAK TO ME:

I'LL CROSS IT, THOUGH IT BLAST ME.
STEP

IF THERE BE ANY GOOD THING TO BE DONE, THAT MAY TO THEE DO EASE AND GRACE TO ME, SPEAK TO ME:
IF THOU ART PRIVY TO THY COUNTRY'S FATE, WHICH, HAPPILY, FOREKNOWING MAY AVOID,
O, SPEAK!

HHHHHHHSHHH

STAY, AND SPEAK!

OR IF THOU HAST UPHOARDED IN THY LIFE EXTORTED TREASURE IN THE WOMB OF EARTH, FOR WHICH, THEY SAY, YOU SPIRITS OFT WALK IN DEATH, SPEAK OF IT:

STOP IT, MARCELLUS.

DO, IF IT WILL NOT STAND.
FWIP
SHALL I STRIKE AT IT WITH MY PARTISAN?
FWSSH

ER-
ER-
ARRAW!

'TIS GONE!

'TIS HERE!
'TIS HERE!

PHWOOO......

AND THEN IT STARTED LIKE A GUILTY THING UPON A FEARFUL SUMMONS. I HAVE HEARD, THE COCK, THAT IS THE TRUMPET TO THE MORN, DOTH WITH HIS LOFTY AND SHRILL-SOUNDING THROAT AWAKE THE GOD OF DAY;

AND, AT HIS WARNING, WHETHER IN SEA OR FIRE, IN EARTH OR AIR, THE EXTRAVAGANT AND ERRING SPIRIT HIES TO HIS CONFINE:

AND OF THE TRUTH HEREIN THIS PRESENT OBJECT MADE PROBATION.

IT WAS ABOUT TO SPEAK, WHEN THE COCK CREW.

WE DO IT WRONG, BEING SO MAJESTICAL, TO OFFER IT THE SHOW OF VIOLENCE;

FOR IT IS, AS THE AIR, INVULNERABLE, AND OUR VAIN BLOWS MALICIOUS MOCKERY.

IT FADED ON THE CROWING OF THE COCK. SOME SAY THAT EVER 'GAINST THAT SEASON COMES WHEREIN OUR SAVIOUR'S BIRTH IS CELEBRATED, THE BIRD OF DAWNING SINGETH ALL NIGHT LONG:
AND THEN, THEY SAY, NO SPIRIT DARES STIR ABROAD; THE NIGHTS ARE WHOLESOME; THEN NO PLANETS STRIKE, NO FAIRY TAKES, NOR WITCH HATH POWER TO CHARM,
SO HALLOW'D AND SO GRACIOUS IS THE TIME.

SO HAVE I HEARD AND DO IN PART BELIEVE IT. BUT, LOOK, THE MORN, IN RUSSET MANTLE CLAD, WALKS O'ER THE DEW OF YON HIGH EASTWARD HILL:

BREAK WE OUR WATCH UP; AND BY MY ADVICE, LET US IMPART WHAT WE HAVE SEEN TO-NIGHT UNTO YOUNG HAMLET; FOR, UPON MY LIFE, THIS SPIRIT, DUMB TO US, WILL SPEAK TO HIM.
DO YOU CONSENT WE SHALL ACQUAINT HIM WITH IT, AS NEEDFUL IN OUR LOVES, FITTING OUR DUTY?
LET'S DO'T, I PRAY; AND I THIS MORNING KNOW WHERE WE SHALL FIND HIM MOST CONVENIENTLY.

THE CASTLE

THOUGH YET OF HAMLET OUR DEAR BROTHER'S DEATH THE MEMORY BE GREEN, AND THAT IT US BEFITTED TO BEAR OUR HEARTS IN GRIEF AND OUR WHOLE KINGDOM TO BE CONTRACTED IN ONE BROW OF WOE,

CLAP! CLAP!

CLAP CLAP CLAP

KING CLAUDIUS

QUEEN GERTRUDE

THEREFORE OUR SOMETIME SISTER, NOW OUR QUEEN, THE IMPERIAL JOINTRESS TO THIS WARLIKE STATE, HAVE WE, AS 'TWERE WITH A DEFEATED JOY - WITH AN AUSPICIOUS AND A DROPPING EYE, WITH MIRTH IN FUNERAL AND WITH DIRGE IN MARRIAGE, IN EQUAL SCALE WEIGHING DELIGHT AND DOLE - TAKEN TO WIFE:
YET SO FAR HATH DISCRETION FOUGHT WITH NATURE THAT WE WITH WISEST SORROW THINK ON HIM, TOGETHER WITH REMEMBRANCE OF OURSELVES.
SHF
NOW FOLLOWS, THAT YOU KNOW,
NOR HAVE WE HEREIN BARR'D YOUR BETTER WISDOMS, WHICH HAVE FREELY GONE WITH THIS AFFAIR ALONG. FOR ALL, OUR THANKS.

YOUNG FORTINBRAS, HOLDING A WEAK SUPPOSAL OF OUR WORTH, OR THINKING BY OUR LATE DEAR BROTHER'S DEATH OUR STATE TO BE DISJOINT AND OUT OF FRAME,
COLLEAGUED WITH THE DREAM OF HIS ADVANTAGE,
HE HATH NOT FAIL'D TO PESTER US WITH MESSAGE, IMPORTING THE SURRENDER OF THOSE LANDS LOST BY HIS FATHER, WITH ALL BONDS OF LAW, TO OUR MOST VALIANT BROTHER.
SO MUCH FOR HIM.
NOW FOR OURSELF AND FOR THIS TIME OF MEETING: THUS MUCH THE BUSINESS IS: WE HAVE HERE WRIT TO NORWAY, UNCLE OF YOUNG FORTINBRAS - WHO, IMPOTENT AND BED-RID, SCARCELY HEARS OF THIS HIS NEPHEW'S PURPOSE -
TO SUPPRESS HIS FURTHER GAIT HEREIN; IN THAT THE LEVIES, THE LISTS AND FULL PROPORTIONS, ARE ALL MADE OUT OF HIS SUBJECT:

FAREWELL, AND LET YOUR HASTE COMMEND YOUR DUTY.
IN THAT AND ALL THINGS WILL WE SHOW OUR DUTY.

VOLTIMAND
CORNELIUS
AND WE HERE DISPATCH YOU, GOOD CORNELIUS, AND YOU, VOLTIMAND, FOR BEARERS OF THIS GREETING TO OLD NORWAY; GIVING TO YOU NO FURTHER PERSONAL POWER TO BUSINESS WITH THE KING, MORE THAN THE SCOPE OF THESE DELATED ARTICLES ALLOW.

EH?

WE DOUBT IT NOTHING: HEARTILY FAREWELL.

AND NOW, LAERTES, WHAT'S THE NEWS WITH YOU? YOU TOLD US OF SOME SUIT; WHAT IS'T, LAERTES? YOU CANNOT SPEAK OF REASON TO THE DANE, AND LOOSE YOUR VOICE:

WHAT WOULDST THOU BEG, LAERTES, THAT SHALL NOT BE MY OFFER, NOT THY ASKING?

TMP

THE HEAD IS NOT MORE NATIVE TO THE HEART, THE HAND MORE INSTRUMENTAL TO THE MOUTH, THAN IS THE THRONE OF DENMARK TO THY FATHER.

WHAT WOULDST THOU HAVE, LAERTES?

MY DREAD LORD, YOUR LEAVE AND FAVOUR TO RETURN TO FRANCE; FROM WHENCE THOUGH WILLINGLY I CAME TO DENMARK, TO SHOW MY DUTY IN YOUR CORONATION,

YET NOW, I MUST CONFESS, THAT DUTY DONE, MY THOUGHTS AND WISHES BEND AGAIN TOWARD FRANCE AND BOW THEM TO YOUR GRACIOUS LEAVE AND PARDON.

BOW~
TAKE THY FAIR HOUR, LAERTES; TIME BE THINE, AND THY BEST GRACES SPEND IT AT THY WILL!
SHUF
BUT NOW, MY COUSIN HAMLET, AND MY SON -
A LITTLE MORE THAN KIN,

AND LESS
THAN KIND.
HAMLET

HOW IS IT THAT THE CLOUDS STILL HANG ON YOU?

NOT SO, MY LORD; I AM TOO MUCH I' THE SUN.

RRR

GOOD HAMLET, CAST THY NIGHTED COLOUR OFF, AND LET THINE EYE LOOK LIKE A FRIEND ON DENMARK.

AY, MADAM, IT IS COMMON.

DO NOT FOR EVER WITH THY VAILED LIDS SEEK FOR THY NOBLE FATHER IN THE DUST:
THOU KNOW'ST 'TIS COMMON; ALL THAT LIVES MUST DIE, PASSING THROUGH NATURE TO ETERNITY.

IF IT BE, WHY SEEMS IT SO PARTICULAR WITH THEE?

I KNOW NOT 'SEEMS.'

SEEMS, MADAM! NAY IT IS;

'TIS NOT ALONE MY INKY CLOAK, GOOD MOTHER, NOR CUSTOMARY SUITS OF SOLEMN BLACK, NOR WINDY SUSPIRATION OF FORCED BREATH,
NO, NOR THE FRUITFUL RIVER IN THE EYE, NOR THE DEJECTED 'HAVIOR OF THE VISAGE, TOGETHER WITH ALL FORMS, MOODS, SHAPES OF GRIEF, THAT CAN DENOTE ME TRULY:
THESE INDEED SEEM, FOR THEY ARE ACTIONS THAT A MAN MIGHT PLAY:
BUT I HAVE THAT WITHIN WHICH PASSETH SHOW; THESE BUT THE TRAPPINGS AND THE SUITS OF WOE.

BUT, YOU MUST KNOW, YOUR FATHER LOST A FATHER; THAT FATHER LOST, LOST HIS,

'TIS SWEET AND COMMENDABLE IN YOUR NATURE, HAMLET, TO GIVE THESE MOURNING DUTIES TO YOUR FATHER:

AND THE SURVIVOR BOUND IN FILIAL OBLIGATION FOR SOME TERM TO DO OBSEQUIOUS SORROW:

BUT TO PERSEVER IN OBSTINATE CONDOLEMENT IS A COURSE OF IMPIOUS STUBBORNNESS; 'TIS UNMANLY GRIEF; IT SHOWS A WILL MOST INCORRECT TO HEAVEN,

A HEART UNFORTIFIED, A MIND IMPATIENT, AN UNDERSTANDING SIMPLE AND UNSCHOOL'D:

FOR WHAT WE KNOW MUST BE AND IS AS COMMON AS ANY THE MOST VULGAR THING TO SENSE, WHY SHOULD WE IN OUR PEEVISH OPPOSITION TAKE IT TO HEART?

FIE! 'TIS A FAULT TO HEAVEN, A FAULT AGAINST THE DEAD, A FAULT TO NATURE, TO REASON MOST ABSURD: WHOSE COMMON THEME IS DEATH OF FATHERS, AND WHO STILL HATH CRIED, FROM THE FIRST CORSE TILL HE THAT DIED TO-DAY, 'THIS MUST BE SO.'
WE PRAY YOU, THROW TO EARTH THIS UNPREVAILING WOE, AND THINK OF US AS OF A FATHER: FOR LET THE WORLD TAKE NOTE, YOU ARE THE MOST IMMEDIATE TO OUR THRONE;
PAT
AND WITH NO LESS NOBILITY OF LOVE THAN THAT WHICH DEAREST FATHER BEARS HIS SON, DO I IMPART TOWARD YOU.
SIGH

LET NOT THY MOTHER LOSE HER PRAYERS, HAMLET: I PRAY THEE, STAY WITH US; GO NOT TO WITTENBERG.

FOR YOUR INTENT IN GOING BACK TO SCHOOL IN WITTENBERG, IT IS MOST RETROGRADE TO OUR DESIRE:

AND WE BESEECH YOU, BEND YOU TO REMAIN HERE, IN THE CHEER AND COMFORT OF OUR EYE, OUR CHIEFEST COURTIER, COUSIN, AND OUR SON.

...

I SHALL IN ALL MY BEST OBEY YOU, MADAM.

MADAM, COME;
WHY, 'TIS A LOVING AND A FAIR REPLY: BE AS OURSELF IN DENMARK.

THIS GENTLE AND UNFORCED ACCORD OF HAMLET SITS SMILING TO MY HEART: IN GRACE WHEREOF, NO JOCUND HEALTH THAT DENMARK DRINKS TO-DAY, BUT THE GREAT CANNON TO THE CLOUDS SHALL TELL,

AND THE KING'S ROUSE THE HEAVENS ALL BRUIT AGAIN, RE-SPEAKING EARTHLY THUNDER.
COME AWAY.
SHUF

O, THAT THIS TOO TOO SOLID FLESH WOULD MELT, THAW, AND RESOLVE ITSELF INTO A DEW!
OR THAT THE EVERLASTING HAD NOT FIX'D HIS CANON 'GAINST SELF-SLAUGHTER!
O GOD! GOD! HOW WEARY, STALE, FLAT AND UNPROFITABLE, SEEM TO ME ALL THE USES OF THIS WORLD!

FIE ON'T!
AH FIE! 'TIS AN UNWEEDED GARDEN, THAT GROWS TO SEED; THINGS RANK AND GROSS IN NATURE POSSESS IT MERELY.
THAT IT SHOULD COME TO THIS! BUT TWO MONTHS DEAD:
NAY, NOT SO MUCH, NOT TWO:
SO EXCELLENT A KING; THAT WAS, TO THIS, HYPERION TO A SATYR;
RRRG-!

SO LOVING TO MY MOTHER THAT HE MIGHT NOT BETEEM THE WINDS OF HEAVEN VISIT HER FACE TOO ROUGHLY.
HEAVEN AND EARTH! MUST I REMEMBER?
WHY, SHE WOULD HANG ON HIM, AS IF INCREASE OF APPETITE HAD GROWN BY WHAT IT FED ON:
AND YET, WITHIN A MONTH - LET ME NOT THINK ON'T.
- FRAILTY, THY NAME IS WOMAN! -

A LITTLE MONTH, OR ERE THOSE SHOES WERE OLD WITH WHICH SHE FOLLOW'D MY POOR FATHER'S BODY, LIKE NIOBE, ALL TEARS - WHY SHE, EVEN SHE -
O, GOD! A BEAST, THAT WANTS DISCOURSE OF REASON, WOULD HAVE MOURN'D LONGER -
MARRIED WITH MY UNCLE,
MY FATHER'S BROTHER, BUT NO MORE LIKE MY FATHER THAN I TO HERCULES.

HAIL TO YOUR LORDSHIP!
TMP TMP
I AM GLAD TO SEE YOU WELL: HORATIO -
OR I DO FORGET MYSELF.
WITHIN A MONTH? ERE YET THE SALT OF MOST UNRIGHTEOUS TEARS HAD LEFT THE FLUSHING IN HER GALLED EYES, SHE MARRIED.
O, MOST WICKED SPEED, TO POST WITH SUCH DEXTERITY TO INCESTUOUS SHEETS! IT IS NOT NOR IT CANNOT COME TO GOOD:
BUT BREAK, MY HEART; FOR I MUST HOLD MY TONGUE.

THE SAME, MY LORD, AND YOUR POOR SERVANT EVER.

SIR, MY GOOD FRIEND; I'LL CHANGE THAT NAME WITH YOU:

AND WHAT MAKE YOU FROM WITTENBERG, HORATIO?

AH!

MARCELLUS?

MY GOOD LORD -

I WOULD NOT HEAR YOUR ENEMY SAY SO, NOR SHALL YOU DO MINE EAR THAT VIOLENCE, TO MAKE IT TRUSTER OF YOUR OWN REPORT AGAINST YOURSELF:

BUT WHAT, IN FAITH, MAKE YOU FROM WITTENBERG?

A TRUANT DISPOSITION, GOOD MY LORD.

I KNOW YOU ARE NO TRUANT. BUT WHAT IS YOUR AFFAIR IN ELSINORE? WE'LL TEACH YOU TO DRINK DEEP ERE YOU DEPART.

FWUMP!

AUGH!
I PRAY THEE, DO NOT MOCK ME, FELLOW-STUDENT; I THINK IT WAS TO SEE MY MOTHER'S WEDDING.
INDEED, MY LORD, IT FOLLOW'D HARD UPON.
MY LORD, I CAME TO SEE YOUR FATHER'S FUNERAL.

MY FATHER! - METHINKS I SEE MY FATHER.
WHERE, MY LORD?
WHA?
THRIFT, THRIFT, HORATIO! THE FUNERAL BAKED MEATS DID COLDLY FURNISH FORTH THE MARRIAGE TABLES.
WOULD I HAD MET MY DEAREST FOE IN HEAVEN OR EVER I HAD SEEN THAT DAY, HORATIO!

IN MY MIND'S EYE, HORATIO.
PO
I SAW HIM ONCE; HE WAS A GOODLY KING.
HE WAS A MAN, TAKE HIM FOR ALL IN ALL, I SHALL NOT LOOK UPON HIS LIKE AGAIN.
MY LORD, I THINK I SAW HIM YESTERNIGHT.
SAW? WHO?
MY LORD, THE KING YOUR FATHER.
!!!
THE KING MY FATHER!

FOR GOD'S LOVE, LET ME HEAR.
SEASON YOUR ADMIRATION FOR AWHILE WITH AN ATTENT EAR, TILL I MAY DELIVER, UPON THE WITNESS OF THESE GENTLEMEN, THIS MARVEL TO YOU.
TWO NIGHTS TOGETHER HAD THESE GENTLEMEN, MARCELLUS AND BERNARDO, ON THEIR WATCH, IN THE DEAD VAST AND MIDDLE OF THE NIGHT, BEEN THUS ENCOUNTER'D.
A FIGURE LIKE YOUR FATHER, ARMED AT POINT EXACTLY, CAP-A-PE, APPEARS BEFORE THEM, AND WITH SOLEMN MARCH GOES SLOW AND STATELY BY THEM:
THRICE HE WALK'D BY THEIR OPPRESS'D AND FEAR-SURPRISED EYES, WITHIN HIS TRUNCHEON'S LENGTH; WHILST THEY, DISTILLED ALMOST TO JELLY WITH THE ACT OF FEAR, STAND DUMB AND SPEAK NOT TO HIM.
THIS TO ME IN DREADFUL SECRECY IMPART THEY DID; AND I WITH THEM THE THIRD NIGHT KEPT THE WATCH;
WHERE, AS THEY HAD DELIVER'D, BOTH IN TIME, FORM OF THE THING, EACH WORD MADE TRUE AND GOOD, THE APPARITION COMES:
I KNEW YOUR FATHER; THESE HANDS ARE NOT MORE LIKE.
BUT WHERE WAS THIS?

DID YOU NOT SPEAK TO IT?
MY LORD, UPON THE PLATFORM WHERE WE WATCH'D.
MY LORD, I DID; BUT ANSWER MADE IT NONE: YET ONCE METHOUGHT IT LIFTED UP ITS HEAD AND DID ADDRESS ITSELF TO MOTION, LIKE AS IT WOULD SPEAK;
BUT EVEN THEN THE MORNING COCK CREW LOUD, AND AT THE SOUND IT SHRUNK IN HASTE AWAY, AND VANISH'D FROM OUR SIGHT.
'TIS VERY STRANGE.

WE DO, MY LORD.
AS I DO LIVE, MY HONOUR'D LORD, 'TIS TRUE;
AND WE DID THINK IT WRIT DOWN IN OUR DUTY TO LET YOU KNOW OF IT.
INDEED, INDEED, SIRS, BUT THIS TROUBLES ME. HOLD YOU THE WATCH TO-NIGHT?
ARM'D, SAY YOU?
ARM'D, MY LORD.
FROM TOP TO TOE?
MY LORD, FROM HEAD TO FOOT.

THEN SAW YOU NOT HIS FACE?

O, YES, MY LORD; HE WORE HIS BEAVER UP.
WHAT, LOOK'D HE FROWNINGLY?
A COUNTENANCE MORE IN SORROW THAN IN ANGER.
PALE OR RED?

NAY, VERY PALE.

HAAA...
I WOULD I HAD BEEN THERE.
AND FIX'D HIS EYES UPON YOU?
MOST CONSTANTLY.
VERY LIKE, VERY LIKE. STAY'D IT LONG?
IT WOULD HAVE MUCH AMAZED YOU.
WHILE ONE WITH MODERATE HASTE MIGHT TELL A HUNDRED.
LONGER, LONGER.

HIS BEARD WAS GRIZZLED - NO?
IT WAS, AS I HAVE SEEN IT IN HIS LIFE, A SABLE SILVER'D.

NOT WHEN I SAW'T.

IF IT ASSUME MY NOBLE FATHER'S PERSON, I'LL SPEAK TO IT, THOUGH HELL ITSELF SHOULD GAPE AND BID ME HOLD MY PEACE.

I WILL WATCH TO-NIGHT; PERCHANCE 'TWILL WALK AGAIN.
I WARRANT IT WILL.

I PRAY YOU ALL, IF YOU HAVE HITHERTO CONCEAL'D THIS SIGHT, LET IT BE TENABLE IN YOUR SILENCE STILL; AND WHATSOEVER ELSE SHALL HAP TO-NIGHT, GIVE IT AN UNDERSTANDING, BUT NO TONGUE:
I WILL REQUITE YOUR LOVES. SO, FARE YOU WELL: UPON THE PLATFORM, 'TWIXT ELEVEN AND TWELVE, I'LL VISIT YOU.
OUR DUTY TO YOUR HONOUR.
YOUR LOVES, AS MINE TO YOU:
FAREWELL.
TIK
TIK TIK
MY FATHER'S SPIRIT IN ARMS! ALL IS NOT WELL; I DOUBT SOME FOUL PLAY:

WOULD THE NIGHT WERE COME!
TILL THEN SIT STILL, MY SOUL: FOUL DEEDS WILL RISE, THOUGH ALL THE EARTH O'ERWHELM THEM, TO MEN'S EYES.
NNNGH!

ACT I
SCENE III
POLONIUS' HOUSE
MY NECESSARIES ARE EMBARK'D. FAREWELL.
AND, SISTER, AS THE WINDS GIVE BENEFIT AND CONVOY IS ASSISTANT, DO NOT SLEEP, BUT LET ME HEAR FROM YOU.
DO YOU DOUBT THAT?
LAERTES
OPHELIA

FOR HAMLET AND THE TRIFLING OF HIS FAVOUR, HOLD IT A FASHION AND A TOY IN BLOOD,

A VIOLET IN THE YOUTH OF PRIMY NATURE, FORWARD, NOT PERMANENT, SWEET, NOT LASTING, THE PERFUME AND SUPPLIANCE OF A MINUTE; NO MORE.

NO MORE BUT SO?

THINK IT NO MORE;

FOR NATURE, CRESCENT, DOES NOT GROW ALONE IN THEWS AND BULK, BUT, AS THIS TEMPLE WAXES, THE INWARD SERVICE OF THE MIND AND SOUL GROWS WIDE WITHAL.

PERHAPS HE LOVES YOU NOW, AND NOW NO SOIL NOR CAUTEL DOTH BESMIRCH THE VIRTUE OF HIS WILL; BUT YOU MUST FEAR, HIS GREATNESS WEIGH'D, HIS WILL IS NOT HIS OWN; FOR HE HIMSELF IS SUBJECT TO HIS BIRTH:
HE MAY NOT, AS UNVALUED PERSONS DO, CARVE FOR HIMSELF; FOR ON HIS CHOICE DEPENDS THE SAFETY AND HEALTH OF THIS WHOLE STATE;
AND THEREFORE MUST HIS CHOICE BE CIRCUMSCRIBED UNTO THE VOICE AND YIELDING OF THAT BODY WHEREOF HE IS THE HEAD.
THEN IF HE SAYS HE LOVES YOU, IT FITS YOUR WISDOM SO FAR TO BELIEVE IT AS HE IN HIS PARTICULAR ACT AND PLACE MAY GIVE HIS SAYING DEED;
WHICH IS NO FURTHER THAN THE MAIN VOICE OF DENMARK GOES WITHAL.
THEN WEIGH WHAT LOSS YOUR HONOUR MAY SUSTAIN, IF WITH TOO CREDENT EAR YOU LIST HIS SONGS, OR LOSE YOUR HEART, OR YOUR CHASTE TREASURE OPEN TO HIS UNMASTER'D IMPORTUNITY.

FEAR IT, OPHELIA, FEAR IT, MY DEAR SISTER, AND KEEP YOU IN THE REAR OF YOUR AFFECTION, OUT OF THE SHOT AND DANGER OF DESIRE.
THE CHARIEST MAID IS PRODIGAL ENOUGH, IF SHE UNMASK HER BEAUTY TO THE MOON.
VIRTUE ITSELF 'SCAPES NOT CALUMNIOUS STROKES:
THE CANKER GALLS THE INFANTS OF THE SPRING, TOO OFT BEFORE THEIR BUTTONS BE DISCLOSED,
AND IN THE MORN AND LIQUID DEW OF YOUTH CONTAGIOUS BLASTMENTS ARE MOST IMMINENT.
BE WARY THEN; BEST SAFETY LIES IN FEAR. YOUTH TO ITSELF REBELS, THOUGH NONE ELSE NEAR.
PAT
I SHALL THE EFFECT OF THIS GOOD LESSON KEEP AS WATCHMAN TO MY HEART.
BUT, GOOD MY BROTHER,

AHEM
O, FEAR ME NOT. I STAY TOO LONG:
DO NOT, AS SOME UNGRACIOUS PASTORS DO, SHOW ME THE STEEP AND THORNY WAY TO HEAVEN;
WHILES, LIKE A PUFF'D AND RECKLESS LIBERTINE, HIMSELF THE PRIMROSE PATH OF DALLIANCE TREADS, AND RECKS NOT HIS OWN REDE.
BUT HERE MY FATHER COMES.
A DOUBLE BLESSING IS A DOUBLE GRACE, OCCASION SMILES UPON A SECOND LEAVE.
YET HERE, LAERTES! ABOARD, ABOARD, FOR SHAME!
THE WIND SITS IN THE SHOULDER OF YOUR SAIL, AND YOU ARE STAY'D FOR.

MY BLESSING WITH THEE!
THERE;
POLONIUS
AND THESE FEW PRECEPTS IN THY MEMORY SEE THOU CHARACTER. GIVE THY THOUGHTS NO TONGUE, NOR ANY UNPROPORTIONED THOUGHT HIS ACT.
BE THOU FAMILIAR, BUT BY NO MEANS VULGAR. THOSE FRIENDS THOU HAST, AND THEIR ADOPTION TRIED, GRAPPLE THEM TO THY SOUL WITH HOOPS OF STEEL;
BUT DO NOT DULL THY PALM WITH ENTERTAINMENT OF EACH NEW-HATCH'D, UNFLEDGED COMRADE.
BEWARE OF ENTRANCE TO A QUARREL, BUT BEING IN, BEAR'T THAT THE OPPOSED MAY BEWARE OF THEE.

GIVE EVERY MAN THY EAR, BUT FEW THY VOICE;
TAKE EACH MAN'S CENSURE, BUT RESERVE THY JUDGMENT.
COSTLY THY HABIT AS THY PURSE CAN BUY, BUT NOT EXPRESS'D IN FANCY; RICH, NOT GAUDY;
FOR THE APPAREL OFT PROCLAIMS THE MAN, AND THEY IN FRANCE OF THE BEST RANK AND STATION ARE OF A MOST SELECT AND GENEROUS CHIEF IN THAT.
UM...
NEITHER A BORROWER NOR A LENDER BE; FOR LOAN OFT LOSES BOTH ITSELF AND FRIEND; AND BORROWING DULLS THE EDGE OF HUSBANDRY.
NYAH
MMPH...

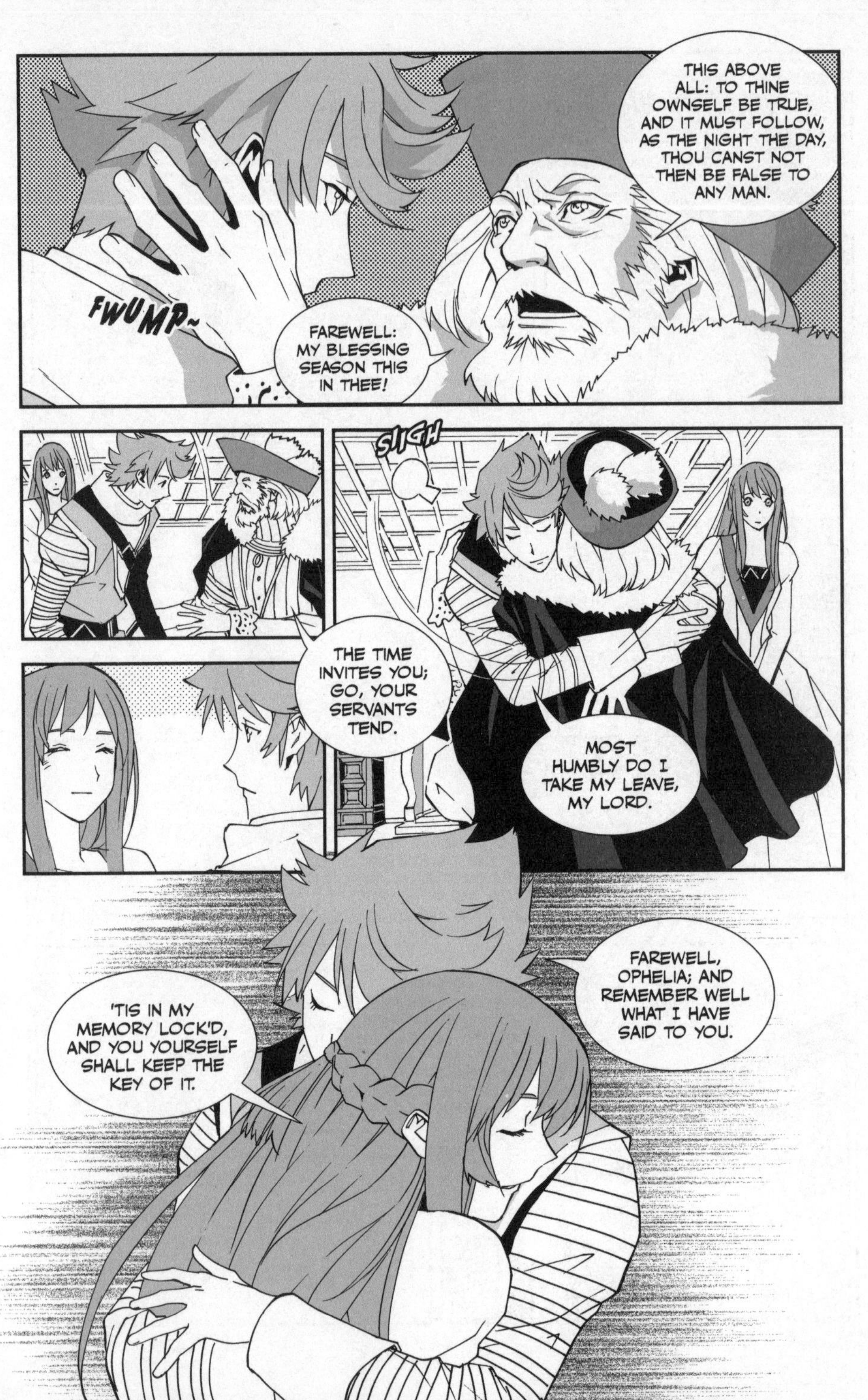

THIS ABOVE ALL: TO THINE OWNSELF BE TRUE, AND IT MUST FOLLOW, AS THE NIGHT THE DAY, THOU CANST NOT THEN BE FALSE TO ANY MAN.
FWUMP~
FAREWELL: MY BLESSING SEASON THIS IN THEE!
SIIGH
THE TIME INVITES YOU; GO, YOUR SERVANTS TEND.
MOST HUMBLY DO I TAKE MY LEAVE, MY LORD.
FAREWELL, OPHELIA; AND REMEMBER WELL WHAT I HAVE SAID TO YOU.
'TIS IN MY MEMORY LOCK'D, AND YOU YOURSELF SHALL KEEP THE KEY OF IT.

FAREWELL.

CLIK.

HE HATH SAID TO YOU?

WHAT IS'T, OPHELIA,

SO PLEASE YOU, SOMETHING TOUCHING THE LORD HAMLET.
MARRY, WELL BETHOUGHT: 'TIS TOLD ME, HE HATH VERY OFT OF LATE GIVEN PRIVATE TIME TO YOU;
AND YOU YOURSELF HAVE OF YOUR AUDIENCE BEEN MOST FREE AND BOUNTEOUS.
IF IT BE SO, AS SO 'TIS PUT ON ME, AND THAT IN WAY OF CAUTION, I MUST TELL YOU, YOU DO NOT UNDERSTAND YOURSELF SO CLEARLY AS IT BEHOVES MY DAUGHTER AND YOUR HONOUR.
WHAT IS BETWEEN YOU? GIVE ME UP THE TRUTH.
HE HATH, MY LORD, OF LATE MADE MANY TENDERS OF HIS AFFECTION TO ME.

AFFECTION! POOH! YOU SPEAK LIKE A GREEN GIRL, UNSIFTED IN SUCH PERILOUS CIRCUMSTANCE.
DO YOU BELIEVE HIS TENDERS, AS YOU CALL THEM?
I DO NOT KNOW, MY LORD, WHAT I SHOULD THINK.
MARRY, I'LL TEACH YOU: THINK YOURSELF A BABY; THAT YOU HAVE TA'EN THESE TENDERS FOR TRUE PAY, WHICH ARE NOT STERLING.
TENDER YOURSELF MORE DEARLY; OR - NOT TO CRACK THE WIND OF THE POOR PHRASE, RUNNING IT THUS - YOU'LL TENDER ME A FOOL.

MY LORD, HE HATH IMPORTUNED ME WITH LOVE IN HONOURABLE FASHION.
AY, FASHION YOU MAY CALL IT; GO TO, GO TO.
AND HATH GIVEN COUNTENANCE TO HIS SPEECH, MY LORD, WITH ALMOST ALL THE HOLY VOWS OF HEAVEN.

AY, SPRINGES TO CATCH WOODCOCKS. I DO KNOW, WHEN THE BLOOD BURNS, HOW PRODIGAL THE SOUL LENDS THE TONGUE VOWS: THESE BLAZES, DAUGHTER,
EHEH
GIVING MORE LIGHT THAN HEAT, EXTINCT IN BOTH, EVEN IN THEIR PROMISE, AS IT IS A-MAKING, YOU MUST NOT TAKE FOR FIRE.
FROM THIS TIME BE SOMEWHAT SCANTER OF YOUR MAIDEN PRESENCE; SET YOUR ENTREATMENTS AT A HIGHER RATE THAN A COMMAND TO PARLEY.
FOR LORD HAMLET, BELIEVE SO MUCH IN HIM, THAT HE IS YOUNG AND WITH A LARGER TETHER MAY HE WALK THAN MAY BE GIVEN YOU:
IN FEW, OPHELIA, DO NOT BELIEVE HIS VOWS; FOR THEY ARE BROKERS, NOT OF THAT DYE WHICH THEIR INVESTMENTS SHOW, BUT MERE IMPLORATORS OF UNHOLY SUITS, BREATHING LIKE SANCTIFIED AND PIOUS BAWDS, THE BETTER TO BEGUILE.
THIS IS FOR ALL: I WOULD NOT, IN PLAIN TERMS, FROM THIS TIME FORTH, HAVE YOU SO SLANDER ANY MOMENT LEISURE, AS TO GIVE WORDS OR TALK WITH THE LORD HAMLET.

LOOK TO'T, I CHARGE YOU: COME YOUR WAYS.

I SHALL OBEY, MY LORD.

ACT I SCENE IV

THE PLATFORM

THE AIR BITES SHREWDLY; IT IS VERY COLD.

SHIVER~

IT IS A NIPPING AND AN EAGER AIR.

WHAT HOUR NOW?
I THINK IT LACKS OF TWELVE.
NO, IT IS STRUCK.
INDEED? I HEARD IT NOT: THEN IT DRAWS NEAR THE SEASON WHEREIN THE SPIRIT HELD HIS WONT TO WALK.
BOM BOM BOM
TWEEEEEN
WHAT DOES THIS MEAN, MY LORD?
THE KING DOTH WAKE TO-NIGHT AND TAKES HIS ROUSE, KEEPS WASSAIL, AND THE SWAGGERING UP-SPRING REELS; AND, AS HE DRAINS HIS DRAUGHTS OF RHENISH DOWN, THE KETTLE-DRUM AND TRUMPET THUS BRAY OUT THE TRIUMPH OF HIS PLEDGE.
HO!
HO!

IS IT A CUSTOM?
AY, MARRY, IS'T: BUT TO MY MIND, THOUGH I AM NATIVE HERE AND TO THE MANNER BORN, IT IS A CUSTOM MORE HONOUR'D IN THE BREACH THAN THE OBSERVANCE.
THIS HEAVY-HEADED REVEL EAST AND WEST MAKES US TRADUCED AND TAX'D OF OTHER NATIONS: THEY CLEPE US DRUNKARDS, AND WITH SWINISH PHRASE SOIL OUR ADDITION; AND INDEED IT TAKES FROM OUR ACHIEVEMENTS, THOUGH PERFORM'D AT HEIGHT, THE PITH AND MARROW OF OUR ATTRIBUTE.
CRAK!!
SO, OFT IT CHANCES IN PARTICULAR MEN, THAT FOR SOME VICIOUS MOLE OF NATURE IN THEM, AS, IN THEIR BIRTH - WHEREIN THEY ARE NOT GUILTY, SINCE NATURE CANNOT CHOOSE HIS ORIGIN -
BY THE O'ERGROWTH OF SOME COMPLEXION, OFT BREAKING DOWN THE PALES AND FORTS OF REASON, OR BY SOME HABIT THAT TOO MUCH O'ER-LEAVENS THE FORM OF PLAUSIVE MANNERS,

THAT THESE MEN, CARRYING, I SAY, THE STAMP OF ONE DEFECT, BEING NATURE'S LIVERY, OR FORTUNE'S STAR - THEIR VIRTUES ELSE - BE THEY AS PURE AS GRACE, AS INFINITE AS MAN MAY UNDERGO - SHALL IN THE GENERAL CENSURE TAKE CORRUPTION FROM THAT PARTICULAR FAULT.

THE DRAM OF EVIL DOTH ALL THE NOBLE SUBSTANCE OF A DOUBT TO HIS OWN SCANDAL.

UM

MM..

ANGELS AND MINISTERS OF GRACE DEFEND US!

HUP!

LOOK, MY LORD, IT COMES!

OH!

AH!

WHOOO..

WHOOOO~

I'LL CALL THEE HAMLET, KING, FATHER, ROYAL DANE.
O, ANSWER ME!
LET ME NOT BURST IN IGNORANCE; BUT TELL WHY THY CANONIZED BONES, HEARSED IN DEATH, HAVE BURST THEIR CEREMENTS;
WHY THE SEPULCHRE, WHEREIN WE SAW THEE QUIETLY INURN'D, HATH OPED HIS PONDEROUS AND MARBLE JAWS, TO CAST THEE UP AGAIN!
SH-SHUF

WHAT MAY THIS MEAN, THAT THOU, DEAD CORSE, AGAIN IN COMPLETE STEEL REVISIT'ST THUS THE GLIMPSES OF THE MOON, MAKING NIGHT HIDEOUS; AND WE FOOLS OF NATURE SO HORRIDLY TO SHAKE OUR DISPOSITION WITH THOUGHTS BEYOND THE REACHES OF OUR SOULS?
SAY, WHY IS THIS? WHEREFORE? WHAT SHOULD WE DO?
TWITCH TWITCH
IT BECKONS YOU TO GO AWAY WITH IT, AS IF IT SOME IMPARTMENT DID DESIRE TO YOU ALONE.

NO, BY NO MEANS.
LOOK, WITH WHAT COURTEOUS ACTION IT WAVES YOU TO A MORE REMOVED GROUND: BUT DO NOT GO WITH IT.
IT WILL NOT SPEAK; THEN I WILL FOLLOW IT.
DO NOT, MY LORD.
WHY, WHAT SHOULD BE THE FEAR? I DO NOT SET MY LIFE IN A PIN'S FEE; AND FOR MY SOUL, WHAT CAN IT DO TO THAT, BEING A THING IMMORTAL AS ITSELF?

WHAT IF IT TEMPT YOU TOWARD THE FLOOD, MY LORD,
IT WAVES ME FORTH AGAIN: I'LL FOLLOW IT.
OR TO THE DREADFUL SUMMIT OF THE CLIFF THAT BEETLES O'ER HIS BASE INTO THE SEA, AND THERE ASSUME SOME OTHER HORRIBLE FORM, WHICH MIGHT DEPRIVE YOUR SOVEREIGNTY OF REASON AND DRAW YOU INTO MADNESS?
THINK OF IT.
THE VERY PLACE PUTS TOYS OF DESPERATION, WITHOUT MORE MOTIVE, INTO EVERY BRAIN THAT LOOKS SO MANY FATHOMS TO THE SEA AND HEARS IT ROAR BENEATH.

GO ON; I'LL FOLLOW THEE.
AH!
IT WAVES ME STILL.
STEP

YOU SHALL NOT GO, MY LORD.

BE RULED; YOU SHALL NOT GO.

HOLD OFF YOUR HANDS.

CLUTCH

MY FATE CRIES OUT, AND MAKES EACH PETTY ARTERY IN THIS BODY AS HARDY AS THE NEMEAN LION'S NERVE.

TWITCH
STILL AM I CALL'D. UNHAND ME, GENTLEMEN.
SHING-
BY HEAVEN, I'LL MAKE A GHOST OF HIM THAT LETS ME!
WHUMP
I SAY, AWAY!

HHHH...
GO ON; I'LL FOLLOW THEE.

HE WAXES DESPERATE WITH IMAGINATION.
LET'S FOLLOW; 'TIS NOT FIT THUS TO OBEY HIM.
HAVE AFTER. TO WHAT ISSUE WILL THIS COME?

SOMETHING IS ROTTEN IN THE STATE OF DENMARK.
HEAVEN WILL DIRECT IT.
SCUFF
NAY, LET'S FOLLOW HIM.
SHUF SHUF SHUF
ACT I
SCENE V

WHERE WILT THOU LEAD ME? SPEAK; I'LL GO NO FURTHER.

HAA...

HAA...

HAA...

ANOTHER PART OF THE PLATFORM.

I WILL.

AAH!

MARK ME.

MY HOUR IS ALMOST COME, WHEN I TO SULPHUROUS AND TORMENTING FLAMES MUST RENDER UP MYSELF.
ALAS, POOR GHOST!

PITY ME NOT, BUT LEND THY SERIOUS HEARING TO WHAT I SHALL UNFOLD.

SPEAK; I AM BOUND TO HEAR.

SO ART THOU TO REVENGE, WHEN THOU SHALT HEAR.
WHAT?

I AM THY FATHER'S SPIRIT,
DOOM'D FOR A CERTAIN TERM TO WALK THE NIGHT, AND FOR THE DAY CONFINED TO FAST IN FIRES, TILL THE FOUL CRIMES DONE IN MY DAYS OF NATURE ARE BURNT AND PURGED AWAY.
BUT THAT I AM FORBID TO TELL THE SECRETS OF MY PRISON-HOUSE, I COULD A TALE UNFOLD WHOSE LIGHTEST WORD WOULD HARROW UP THY SOUL,
FREEZE THY YOUNG BLOOD,
MAKE THY TWO EYES, LIKE STARS, START FROM THEIR SPHERES, THY KNOTTED AND COMBINED LOCKS TO PART AND EACH PARTICULAR HAIR TO STAND ON END, LIKE QUILLS UPON THE FRETFUL PORPENTINE:

BUT THIS ETERNAL BLAZON MUST NOT BE TO EARS OF FLESH AND BLOOD.
LIST, LIST, O, LIST! IF THOU DIDST EVER THY DEAR FATHER LOVE -

REVENGE HIS FOUL AND MOST UNNATURAL MURDER.

O GOD!

MURDER!

MURDER MOST FOUL, AS IN THE BEST IT IS;
BUT THIS MOST FOUL, STRANGE AND UNNATURAL.

I FIND THEE APT;

AND DULLER SHOULDST THOU BE THAN THE FAT WEED THAT ROOTS ITSELF IN EASE ON LETHE WHARF, WOULDST THOU NOT STIR IN THIS.

NOW, HAMLET, HEAR:

HASTE ME TO KNOW'T, THAT I, WITH WINGS AS SWIFT AS MEDITATION OR THE THOUGHTS OF LOVE, MAY SWEEP TO MY REVENGE.

'TIS GIVEN OUT THAT, SLEEPING IN MY ORCHARD, A SERPENT STUNG ME;
SO THE WHOLE EAR OF DENMARK IS BY A FORGED PROCESS OF MY DEATH RANKLY ABUSED;
BUT KNOW, THOU NOBLE YOUTH, THE SERPENT THAT DID STING THY FATHER'S LIFE NOW WEARS HIS CROWN.
O MY PROPHETIC SOUL! MY UNCLE!
AY, THAT INCESTUOUS, THAT ADULTERATE BEAST, WITH WITCHCRAFT OF HIS WIT, WITH TRAITOROUS GIFTS -
O WICKED WIT AND GIFTS, THAT HAVE THE POWER SO TO SEDUCE! - WON TO HIS SHAMEFUL LUST THE WILL OF MY MOST SEEMING-VIRTUOUS QUEEN.
O HAMLET, WHAT A FALLING-OFF WAS THERE!

FROM ME, WHOSE LOVE WAS OF THAT DIGNITY THAT IT WENT HAND IN HAND EVEN WITH THE VOW I MADE TO HER IN MARRIAGE, AND TO DECLINE UPON A WRETCH WHOSE NATURAL GIFTS WERE POOR TO THOSE OF MINE!
BUT VIRTUE, AS IT NEVER WILL BE MOVED, THOUGH LEWDNESS COURT IT IN A SHAPE OF HEAVEN,
SO LUST, THOUGH TO A RADIANT ANGEL LINK'D, WILL SATE ITSELF IN A CELESTIAL BED, AND PREY ON GARBAGE.
BUT, SOFT! METHINKS I SCENT THE MORNING AIR; BRIEF LET ME BE.
SLEEPING WITHIN MY ORCHARD, MY CUSTOM ALWAYS OF THE AFTERNOON, UPON MY SECURE HOUR THY UNCLE STOLE,

HSSSS!
PLIP-
WITH JUICE OF CURSED HEBENON IN A VIAL, AND IN THE PORCHES OF MY EARS DID POUR THE LEPEROUS DISTILMENT,
WHOSE EFFECT HOLDS SUCH AN ENMITY WITH BLOOD OF MAN THAT SWIFT AS QUICKSILVER IT COURSES THROUGH THE NATURAL GATES AND ALLEYS OF THE BODY, AND WITH A SUDDEN VIGOUR DOTH POSSET AND CURD,
LIKE EAGER DROPPINGS INTO MILK, THE THIN AND WHOLESOME BLOOD. SO DID IT MINE;
AND A MOST INSTANT TETTER BARK'D ABOUT, MOST LAZAR-LIKE, WITH VILE AND LOATHSOME CRUST, ALL MY SMOOTH BODY.

THUS WAS I, SLEEPING, BY A BROTHER'S HAND OF LIFE, OF CROWN, OF QUEEN, AT ONCE DISPATCH'D:
CUT OFF EVEN IN THE BLOSSOMS OF MY SIN, UNHOUSEL'D, DISAPPOINTED, UNANEL'D, NO RECKONING MADE, BUT SENT TO MY ACCOUNT WITH ALL MY IMPERFECTIONS ON MY HEAD.
O, HORRIBLE! O, HORRIBLE! MOST HORRIBLE! IF THOU HAST NATURE IN THEE, BEAR IT NOT;
LET NOT THE ROYAL BED OF DENMARK BE A COUCH FOR LUXURY AND DAMNED INCEST.
BUT, HOWSOEVER THOU PURSUEST THIS ACT, TAINT NOT THY MIND, NOR LET THY SOUL CONTRIVE AGAINST THY MOTHER AUGHT:
LEAVE HER TO HEAVEN AND TO THOSE THORNS THAT IN HER BOSOM LODGE, TO PRICK AND STING HER.
FARE THEE WELL AT ONCE!
THE GLOW-WORM SHOWS THE MATIN TO BE NEAR, AND 'GINS TO PALE HIS UNEFFECTUAL FIRE.
ADIEU, ADIEU! HAMLET, REMEMBER ME.

O, FIE! HOLD, HOLD, MY HEART;
AND YOU, MY SINEWS, GROW NOT INSTANT OLD, BUT BEAR ME STIFFLY UP.
REMEMBER THEE!
AY, THOU POOR GHOST, WHILE MEMORY HOLDS A SEAT IN THIS DISTRACTED GLOBE.
PHWOOOOON
O ALL YOU HOST OF HEAVEN! O EARTH!
WHAT ELSE? AND SHALL I COUPLE HELL?
REMEMBER THEE!
YEA, FROM THE TABLE OF MY MEMORY I'LL WIPE AWAY ALL TRIVIAL FOND RECORDS, ALL SAWS OF BOOKS, ALL FORMS, ALL PRESSURES PAST, THAT YOUTH AND OBSERVATION COPIED THERE;
AND THY COMMANDMENT ALL ALONE SHALL LIVE WITHIN THE BOOK AND VOLUME OF MY BRAIN, UNMIX'D WITH BASER MATTER:
YES, BY HEAVEN!
POF!
O MOST PERNICIOUS WOMAN! O VILLAIN, VILLAIN, SMILING, DAMNED VILLAIN!
MY TABLES,
- MEET IT IS I SET IT DOWN, THAT ONE MAY SMILE, AND SMILE, AND BE A VILLAIN;
AT LEAST I'M SURE IT MAY BE SO IN DENMARK:

MY LORD, MY LORD -
LORD HAMLET -

SO, UNCLE, THERE YOU ARE.
NOW TO MY WORD; IT IS 'ADIEU, ADIEU! REMEMBER ME.'
I HAVE SWORN 'T.

HEAVEN SECURE HIM!

SO BE IT!

HILLO, HO, HO, MY LORD!

HILLO, HO, HO, BOY! COME, BIRD, COME.

O, WONDERFUL!

HOW IS'T, MY NOBLE LORD?
WHAT NEWS, MY LORD?

GOOD MY LORD, TELL IT.
NO, YOU'LL REVEAL IT.

NOT I, MY LORD, BY HEAVEN.

NOR I, MY LORD.

HOW SAY YOU, THEN, WOULD HEART OF MAN ONCE THINK IT? - BUT YOU'LL BE SECRET?

THERE'S NE'ER A VILLAIN DWELLING IN ALL DENMARK BUT HE'S AN ARRANT KNAVE.
THERE NEEDS NO GHOST, MY LORD, COME FROM THE GRAVE TO TELL US THIS.

AY, BY HEAVEN, MY LORD.

WHY, RIGHT; YOU ARE I' THE RIGHT; AND SO, WITHOUT MORE CIRCUMSTANCE AT ALL, I HOLD IT FIT THAT WE SHAKE HANDS AND PART:
YOU, AS YOUR BUSINESS AND DESIRE SHALL POINT YOU - FOR EVERY MAN HAS BUSINESS AND DESIRE, SUCH AS IT IS -

AND FOR MINE OWN POOR PART, LOOK YOU, I'LL GO PRAY.

THESE ARE BUT WILD AND WHIRLING WORDS, MY LORD.

I'M SORRY THEY OFFEND YOU, HEARTILY; YES, 'FAITH, HEARTILY.

THERE'S NO OFFENCE, MY LORD.

YES, BY SAINT PATRICK, BUT THERE IS, HORATIO, AND MUCH OFFENCE TOO.

TOUCHING THIS VISION HERE, IT IS AN HONEST GHOST, THAT LET ME TELL YOU.

FOR YOUR DESIRE TO KNOW WHAT IS BETWEEN US, O'ERMASTER 'T AS YOU MAY.

AND NOW, GOOD FRIENDS, AS YOU ARE FRIENDS, SCHOLARS AND SOLDIERS, GIVE ME ONE POOR REQUEST.
WHAT IS'T, MY LORD? WE WILL.
NEVER MAKE KNOWN WHAT YOU HAVE SEEN TO-NIGHT.

IN FAITH, MY LORD, NOT I.
TNK
TMP
NOR I, MY LORD, IN FAITH.

INDEED, UPON MY SWORD, INDEED.

UPON MY SWORD.
WE HAVE SWORN, MY LORD, ALREADY.
SHNNNG

SWEAR.
SHHHSHHHH-
HA, HA, BOY! SAY'ST THOU SO?
ART THOU THERE, TRUEPENNY?

GAH!
PROPOSE THE OATH, MY LORD.
COME ON - YOU HEAR THIS FELLOW IN THE CELLARAGE - CONSENT TO SWEAR.

NEVER TO SPEAK OF THIS THAT YOU HAVE SEEN, SWEAR BY MY SWORD.
SHHHHH
SWEAR.
HIC ET UBIQUE?

AND LAY YOUR HANDS AGAIN UPON MY SWORD. NEVER TO SPEAK OF THIS THAT YOU HAVE HEARD, SWEAR BY MY SWORD.

THEN WE'LL SHIFT OUR GROUND. COME HITHER, GENTLEMEN,

SWEAR BY HIS SWORD.

SHHHH

WELL SAID, OLD MOLE!

CANST WORK I' THE EARTH SO FAST?

A WORTHY PIONER! ONCE MORE REMOVE, GOOD FRIENDS.

O DAY AND NIGHT, BUT THIS IS WONDROUS STRANGE!

AND THEREFORE AS A STRANGER GIVE IT WELCOME. THERE ARE MORE THINGS IN HEAVEN AND EARTH, HORATIO,

THAN ARE DREAMT OF IN YOUR PHILOSOPHY.

BUT COME;

SHUF

HERE, AS BEFORE, NEVER, SO HELP YOU MERCY, HOW STRANGE OR ODD SOE'ER I BEAR MYSELF - AS I PERCHANCE HEREAFTER SHALL THINK MEET TO PUT AN ANTIC DISPOSITION ON - THAT YOU, AT SUCH TIMES SEEING ME, NEVER SHALL, WITH ARMS ENCUMBER'D THUS, OR THIS HEADSHAKE,

OR BY PRONOUNCING OF SOME DOUBTFUL PHRASE, AS 'WELL, WELL, WE KNOW,' OR 'WE COULD, AN IF WE WOULD,' OR 'IF WE LIST TO SPEAK,' OR 'THERE BE, AN IF THEY MIGHT,' OR SUCH AMBIGUOUS GIVING OUT, TO NOTE THAT YOU KNOW AUGHT OF ME -

THIS NOT TO DO, SO GRACE AND MERCY AT YOUR MOST NEED HELP YOU, SWEAR.

TMP
TMP

SWEAR.
SHHHHHHH~

REST, REST, PERTURBED SPIRIT!

SHHHHOOOO...

SO, GENTLEMEN, WITH ALL MY LOVE I DO COMMEND ME TO YOU; AND WHAT SO POOR A MAN AS HAMLET IS MAY DO, TO EXPRESS HIS LOVE AND FRIENDING TO YOU, GOD WILLING, SHALL NOT LACK.

LET US GO IN TOGETHER; AND STILL YOUR FINGERS ON YOUR LIPS, I PRAY.

AH!

NAY, COME, LET'S GO TOGETHER.

THE TIME IS OUT OF JOINT. O CURSED SPITE, THAT EVER I WAS BORN TO SET IT RIGHT!

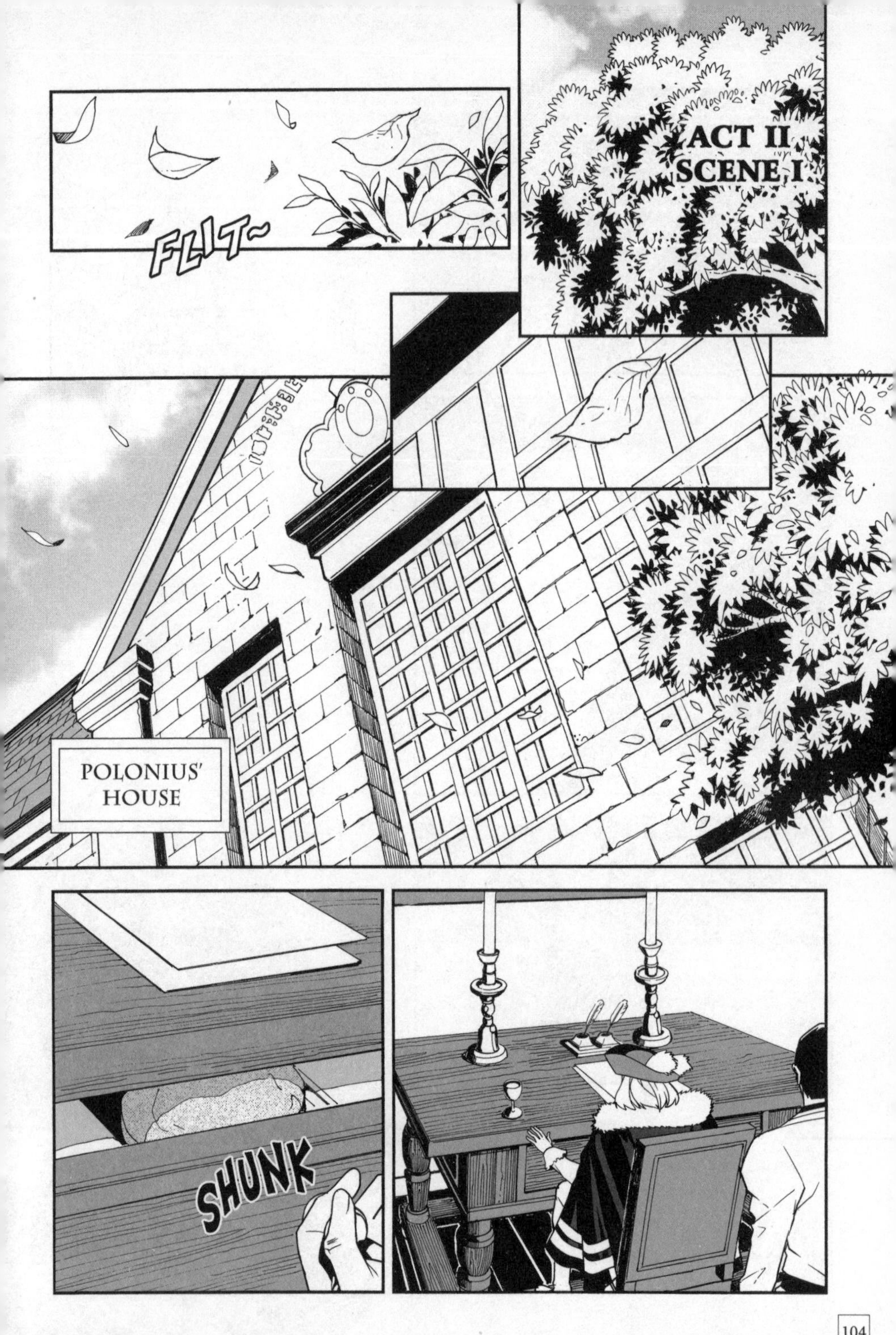

FLIT~

ACT II SCENE I

POLONIUS' HOUSE

YOU SHALL DO MARVELLOUS WISELY, GOOD REYNALDO, BEFORE YOU VISIT HIM, TO MAKE INQUIRE OF HIS BEHAVIOR.

GIVE HIM THIS MONEY AND THESE NOTES, REYNALDO.
I WILL, MY LORD.

MARRY, WELL SAID; VERY WELL SAID.
LOOK YOU, SIR, INQUIRE ME FIRST WHAT DANSKERS ARE IN PARIS;
AND HOW, AND WHO, WHAT MEANS, AND WHERE THEY KEEP, WHAT COMPANY, AT WHAT EXPENSE;

MY LORD, I DID INTEND IT.
CLINK.
REYNALDO

AND FINDING BY THIS ENCOMPASSMENT AND DRIFT OF QUESTION, THAT THEY DO KNOW MY SON, COME YOU MORE NEARER THAN YOUR PARTICULAR DEMANDS WILL TOUCH IT:
TAKE YOU, AS 'TWERE, SOME DISTANT KNOWLEDGE OF HIM; AS THUS, 'I KNOW HIS FATHER AND HIS FRIENDS, AND IN PART HIM:' DO YOU MARK THIS, REYNALDO?
AY, VERY WELL, MY LORD.
MARRY, NONE SO RANK AS MAY DISHONOUR HIM; TAKE HEED OF THAT; BUT, SIR, SUCH WANTON, WILD AND USUAL SLIPS AS ARE COMPANIONS NOTED AND MOST KNOWN TO YOUTH AND LIBERTY.
EH?!
'AND IN PART HIM; BUT,' YOU MAY SAY, 'NOT WELL; BUT, IF'T BE HE I MEAN, HE'S VERY WILD; ADDICTED SO AND SO:' AND THERE PUT ON HIM WHAT FORGERIES YOU PLEASE;

AS GAMING, MY LORD.
AY, OR DRINKING, FENCING, SWEARING, QUARRELLING, DRABBING. YOU MAY GO SO FAR.

MY LORD, THAT WOULD DISHONOUR HIM.

BUT, MY GOOD LORD -

FAITH, NO, AS YOU MAY SEASON IT IN THE CHARGE. YOU MUST NOT PUT ANOTHER SCANDAL ON HIM, THAT HE IS OPEN TO INCONTINENCY; THAT'S NOT MY MEANING:
BUT BREATHE HIS FAULTS SO QUAINTLY THAT THEY MAY SEEM THE TAINTS OF LIBERTY, THE FLASH AND OUTBREAK OF A FIERY MIND, A SAVAGENESS IN UNRECLAIMED BLOOD, OF GENERAL ASSAULT.
GULP

WHEREFORE SHOULD YOU DO THIS?

AY, MY LORD, I WOULD KNOW THAT.

MARRY, SIR, HERE'S MY DRIFT; AND I BELIEVE, IT IS A FETCH OF WIT: YOU LAYING THESE SLIGHT SULLIES ON MY SON, AS 'TWERE A THING A LITTLE SOIL'D I' THE WORKING,

MARK YOU, YOUR PARTY IN CONVERSE, HIM YOU WOULD SOUND, HAVING EVER SEEN IN THE PRENOMINATE CRIMES THE YOUTH YOU BREATHE OF GUILTY,

BE ASSURED HE CLOSES WITH YOU IN THIS CONSEQUENCE; 'GOOD SIR,' OR SO, OR 'FRIEND,' OR 'GENTLEMAN,' ACCORDING TO THE PHRASE OR THE ADDITION OF MAN AND COUNTRY.

SPLISH

BY THE MASS, I WAS ABOUT TO SAY SOMETHING. WHERE DID I LEAVE?

AND THEN, SIR, DOES HE THIS - HE DOES - WHAT WAS I ABOUT TO SAY?

VERY GOOD, MY LORD.

AT 'CLOSES IN THE CONSEQUENCE,' AT 'FRIEND OR SO,' AND 'GENTLEMAN.'

AT 'CLOSES IN THE CONSEQUENCE,' AY, MARRY!

HE CLOSES WITH YOU THUS: 'I KNOW THE GENTLEMAN; I SAW HIM YESTERDAY, OR T' OTHER DAY, OR THEN, OR THEN; WITH SUCH, OR SUCH;'

'AND, AS YOU SAY, THERE WAS A' GAMING; THERE O'ERTOOK IN'S ROUSE; THERE FALLING OUT AT TENNIS:' OR PERCHANCE, 'I SAW HIM ENTER SUCH A HOUSE OF SALE,' VIDELICET, A BROTHEL, OR SO FORTH. SEE YOU NOW;

YOUR BAIT OF FALSEHOOD TAKES THIS CARP OF TRUTH: AND THUS DO WE OF WISDOM AND OF REACH, WITH WINDLASSES AND WITH ASSAYS OF BIAS, BY INDIRECTIONS FIND DIRECTIONS OUT.

WELL, MY LORD.
AND LET HIM PLY HIS MUSIC.

FAREWELL!

PLIP
HOW NOW, OPHELIA! WHAT'S THE MATTER?
O, MY LORD, MY LORD, I HAVE BEEN SO AFFRIGHTED!
TAP
TAP
TAP

WITH WHAT, I' THE NAME OF GOD?
AAH!
MY LORD, AS I WAS SEWING IN MY CLOSET, LORD HAMLET, WITH HIS DOUBLET ALL UNBRACED; NO HAT UPON HIS HEAD; HIS STOCKINGS FOUL'D, UNGARTER'D, AND DOWN-GYVED TO HIS ANKLE;
PALE AS HIS SHIRT, HIS KNEES KNOCKING EACH OTHER, AND WITH A LOOK SO PITEOUS IN PURPORT AS IF HE HAD BEEN LOOSED OUT OF HELL TO SPEAK OF HORRORS - HE COMES BEFORE ME.

WHAT SAID HE?
MY LORD, I DO NOT KNOW; BUT TRULY, I DO FEAR IT.
MAD FOR THY LOVE?
HE TOOK ME BY THE WRIST AND HELD ME HARD; THEN GOES HE TO THE LENGTH OF ALL HIS ARM; AND, WITH HIS OTHER HAND THUS O'ER HIS BROW, HE FALLS TO SUCH PERUSAL OF MY FACE AS HE WOULD DRAW IT. LONG STAY'D HE SO;

AT LAST, A LITTLE SHAKING OF MINE ARM AND THRICE HIS HEAD THUS WAVING UP AND DOWN, HE RAISED A SIGH SO PITEOUS AND PROFOUND AS IT DID SEEM TO SHATTER ALL HIS BULK AND END HIS BEING:
THAT DONE, HE LETS ME GO, AND, WITH HIS HEAD OVER HIS SHOULDER TURN'D, HE SEEM'D TO FIND HIS WAY WITHOUT HIS EYES, FOR OUT O' DOORS HE WENT WITHOUT THEIR HELP, AND TO THE LAST BENDED THEIR LIGHT ON ME.

COME, GO WITH ME. I WILL GO SEEK THE KING. THIS IS THE VERY ECSTASY OF LOVE, WHOSE VIOLENT PROPERTY FORDOES ITSELF,
AND LEADS THE WILL TO DESPERATE UNDERTAKINGS AS OFT AS ANY PASSION UNDER HEAVEN THAT DOES AFFLICT OUR NATURES.
GRAB
I AM SORRY.
WHAT,
HAVE YOU GIVEN HIM ANY HARD WORDS OF LATE?
NO, MY GOOD LORD; BUT, AS YOU DID COMMAND, I DID REPEL HIS LETTERS AND DENIED HIS ACCESS TO ME.

BUT BESHREW MY JEALOUSY! BY HEAVEN, IT IS AS PROPER TO OUR AGE TO CAST BEYOND OURSELVES IN OUR OPINIONS AS IT IS COMMON FOR THE YOUNGER SORT TO LACK DISCRETION.
THAT HATH MADE HIM MAD. I AM SORRY THAT WITH BETTER HEED AND JUDGMENT I HAD NOT QUOTED HIM. I FEAR'D HE DID BUT TRIFLE, AND MEANT TO WRECK THEE.

THIS MUST BE KNOWN, WHICH, BEING KEPT CLOSE, MIGHT MOVE MORE GRIEF TO HIDE THAN HATE TO UTTER LOVE.
COME, GO WE TO THE KING.

ACT II
SCENE II
THE CASTLE

WELCOME, DEAR ROSENCRANTZ AND GUILDENSTERN! MOREOVER THAT WE MUCH DID LONG TO SEE YOU, THE NEED WE HAVE TO USE YOU DID PROVOKE OUR HASTY SENDING.
SOMETHING HAVE YOU HEARD OF HAMLET'S TRANSFORMATION; SO CALL IT, SINCE NOR THE EXTERIOR NOR THE INWARD MAN RESEMBLES THAT IT WAS.
WHAT IT SHOULD BE, MORE THAN HIS FATHER'S DEATH, THAT THUS HATH PUT HIM SO MUCH FROM THE UNDERSTANDING OF HIMSELF, I CANNOT DREAM OF.
I ENTREAT YOU BOTH, THAT, BEING OF SO YOUNG DAYS BROUGHT UP WITH HIM, AND SINCE SO NEIGHBOUR'D TO HIS YOUTH AND HUMOUR, THAT YOU VOUCHSAFE YOUR REST HERE IN OUR COURT SOME LITTLE TIME, SO BY YOUR COMPANIES TO DRAW HIM ON TO PLEASURES, AND TO GATHER,
GUILDENSTERN
ROSENCRANTZ

GOOD GENTLEMEN, HE HATH MUCH TALK'D OF YOU; AND SURE I AM TWO MEN THERE ARE NOT LIVING TO WHOM HE MORE ADHERES.

SO MUCH AS FROM OCCASION YOU MAY GLEAN, WHETHER AUGHT, TO US UNKNOWN, AFFLICTS HIM THUS, THAT, OPEN'D, LIES WITHIN OUR REMEDY.

IF IT WILL PLEASE YOU TO SHOW US SO MUCH GENTRY AND GOOD WILL AS TO EXPEND YOUR TIME WITH US AWHILE,
FOR THE SUPPLY AND PROFIT OF OUR HOPE, YOUR VISITATION SHALL RECEIVE SUCH THANKS AS FITS A KING'S REMEMBRANCE.

BOTH YOUR MAJESTIES MIGHT, BY THE SOVEREIGN POWER YOU HAVE OF US, PUT YOUR DREAD PLEASURES MORE INTO COMMAND THAN TO ENTREATY.

THANKS, ROSENCRANTZ AND GENTLE GUILDENSTERN.
BUT WE BOTH OBEY, AND HERE GIVE UP OURSELVES, IN THE FULL BENT TO LAY OUR SERVICE FREELY AT YOUR FEET, TO BE COMMANDED.
GO, SOME OF YOU, AND BRING THESE GENTLEMEN WHERE HAMLET IS.
THANKS, GUILDENSTERN AND GENTLE ROSENCRANTZ. AND I BESEECH YOU INSTANTLY TO VISIT MY TOO MUCH CHANGED SON.

AY, AMEN!

HEAVENS MAKE OUR PRESENCE AND OUR PRACTICES PLEASANT AND HELPFUL TO HIM!

FMP

EH?

THE AMBASSADORS FROM NORWAY, MY GOOD LORD, ARE JOYFULLY RETURN'D.

HAVE I, MY LORD? I ASSURE MY GOOD LIEGE, I HOLD MY DUTY, AS I HOLD MY SOUL, BOTH TO MY GOD AND TO MY GRACIOUS KING:
THOU STILL HAST BEEN THE FATHER OF GOOD NEWS.
AND I DO THINK - OR ELSE THIS BRAIN OF MINE HUNTS NOT THE TRAIL OF POLICY SO SURE AS IT HATH USED TO DO - THAT I HAVE FOUND THE VERY CAUSE OF HAMLET'S LUNACY.
O, SPEAK OF THAT; THAT DO I LONG TO HEAR.
GIVE FIRST ADMITTANCE TO THE AMBASSADORS; MY NEWS SHALL BE THE FRUIT TO THAT GREAT FEAST.
THYSELF DO GRACE TO THEM, AND BRING THEM IN.

HE TELLS ME, MY DEAR GERTRUDE, HE HATH FOUND THE HEAD AND SOURCE OF ALL YOUR SON'S DISTEMPER.
I DOUBT IT IS NO OTHER BUT THE MAIN; HIS FATHER'S DEATH, AND OUR O'ERHASTY MARRIAGE.
WELL, WE SHALL SIFT HIM.

WELCOME, MY GOOD FRIENDS!
SAY, VOLTIMAND, WHAT FROM OUR BROTHER NORWAY?
SHUF!
MOST FAIR RETURN OF GREETINGS AND DESIRES. UPON OUR FIRST, HE SENT OUT TO SUPPRESS HIS NEPHEW'S LEVIES, WHICH TO HIM APPEAR'D TO BE A PREPARATION 'GAINST THE POLACK;
BUT, BETTER LOOK'D INTO, HE TRULY FOUND IT WAS AGAINST YOUR HIGHNESS;
WHEREAT GRIEVED, THAT SO HIS SICKNESS, AGE AND IMPOTENCE WAS FALSELY BORNE IN HAND, SENDS OUT ARRESTS ON FORTINBRAS;
WHICH HE, IN BRIEF, OBEYS; RECEIVES REBUKE FROM NORWAY, AND IN FINE MAKES VOW BEFORE HIS UNCLE NEVER MORE TO GIVE THE ASSAY OF ARMS AGAINST YOUR MAJESTY.

WITH AN ENTREATY, HEREIN FURTHER SHOWN, THAT IT MIGHT PLEASE YOU TO GIVE QUIET PASS THROUGH YOUR DOMINIONS FOR THIS ENTERPRISE, ON SUCH REGARDS OF SAFETY AND ALLOWANCE AS THEREIN ARE SET DOWN.
WHEREON OLD NORWAY, OVERCOME WITH JOY, GIVES HIM THREE THOUSAND CROWNS IN ANNUAL FEE, AND HIS COMMISSION TO EMPLOY THOSE SOLDIERS, SO LEVIED AS BEFORE, AGAINST THE POLACK:
IT LIKES US WELL;
AND AT OUR MORE CONSIDER'D TIME WE'LL READ, ANSWER, AND THINK UPON THIS BUSINESS.
MEANTIME WE THANK YOU FOR YOUR WELL-TOOK LABOUR. GO TO YOUR REST; AT NIGHT WE'LL FEAST TOGETHER.
MOST WELCOME HOME!
THIS BUSINESS IS WELL ENDED.
BOW~

MY LIEGE, AND MADAM, TO EXPOSTULATE WHAT MAJESTY SHOULD BE, WHAT DUTY IS,

WHY DAY IS DAY, NIGHT NIGHT, AND TIME IS TIME, WERE NOTHING BUT TO WASTE NIGHT, DAY AND TIME.
THEREFORE, SINCE BREVITY IS THE SOUL OF WIT, AND TEDIOUSNESS THE LIMBS AND OUTWARD FLOURISHES, I WILL BE BRIEF.
YOUR NOBLE SON IS MAD.
MAD CALL I IT; FOR, TO DEFINE TRUE MADNESS, WHAT IS'T BUT TO BE NOTHING ELSE BUT MAD?
BUT LET THAT GO.

MADAM, I SWEAR I USE NO ART AT ALL.
THAT HE IS MAD, 'TIS TRUE: 'TIS TRUE 'TIS PITY; AND PITY 'TIS 'TIS TRUE. A FOOLISH FIGURE; BUT FAREWELL IT, FOR I WILL USE NO ART.

MORE MATTER, WITH LESS ART.

MAD LET US GRANT HIM, THEN: AND NOW REMAINS THAT WE FIND OUT THE CAUSE OF THIS EFFECT, OR RATHER SAY, THE CAUSE OF THIS DEFECT, FOR THIS EFFECT DEFECTIVE COMES BY CAUSE.

OH...
THUS IT REMAINS, AND THE REMAINDER THUS. PERPEND.
I HAVE A DAUGHTER - HAVE WHILE SHE IS MINE - WHO, IN HER DUTY AND OBEDIENCE, MARK, HATH GIVEN ME THIS: NOW GATHER, AND SURMISE.
FWIP
'TO THE CELESTIAL AND MY SOUL'S IDOL, THE MOST BEAUTIFIED OPHELIA,' -
FLAP-

OH NO...
'IN HER EXCELLENT WHITE BOSOM, THESE, ETC.'
THAT'S AN ILL PHRASE, A VILE PHRASE; 'BEAUTIFIED' IS A VILE PHRASE: BUT YOU SHALL HEAR. THUS:
CAME THIS FROM HAMLET TO HER?

GOOD MADAM, STAY AWHILE; I WILL BE FAITHFUL.
HAMLET.

THIS, IN OBEDIENCE, HATH MY DAUGHTER SHOWN ME, AND MORE ABOVE, HATH HIS SOLICITINGS, AS THEY FELL OUT BY TIME, BY MEANS AND PLACE, ALL GIVEN TO MINE EAR.
BUT HOW HATH SHE RECEIVED HIS LOVE?
WHAT DO YOU THINK OF ME?
AS OF A MAN FAITHFUL AND HONOURABLE.
I WOULD FAIN PROVE SO.
'DOUBT THOU THE STARS ARE FIRE;'
'DOUBT THAT THE SUN DOTH MOVE;'
'DOUBT TRUTH TO BE A LIAR;'
'BUT NEVER DOUBT I LOVE.'
'O DEAR OPHELIA, I AM ILL AT THESE NUMBERS. I HAVE NOT ART TO RECKON MY GROANS. BUT THAT I LOVE THEE BEST, O MOST BEST, BELIEVE IT. ADIEU.'
'THINE EVERMORE MOST DEAR LADY, WHILST THIS MACHINE IS TO HIM,
HAMLET.'

BUT WHAT MIGHT YOU THINK, WHEN I HAD SEEN THIS HOT LOVE ON THE WING - AS I PERCEIVED IT, I MUST TELL YOU THAT, BEFORE MY DAUGHTER TOLD ME - WHAT MIGHT YOU,
OR MY DEAR MAJESTY YOUR QUEEN HERE, THINK, IF I HAD PLAY'D THE DESK OR TABLE-BOOK, OR GIVEN MY HEART A WINKING, MUTE AND DUMB, OR LOOK'D UPON THIS LOVE WITH IDLE SIGHT, WHAT MIGHT YOU THINK?
NO, I WENT ROUND TO WORK, AND MY YOUNG MISTRESS THUS I DID BESPEAK:
'LORD HAMLET IS A PRINCE, OUT OF THY STAR; THIS MUST NOT BE.'

AND THEN I PRECEPTS GAVE HER, THAT SHE SHOULD LOCK HERSELF FROM HIS RESORT, ADMIT NO MESSENGERS, RECEIVE NO TOKENS.
WHICH DONE, SHE TOOK THE FRUITS OF MY ADVICE; AND HE, REPULSED - A SHORT TALE TO MAKE -
FELL INTO A SADNESS, THEN INTO A FAST, THENCE TO A WATCH, THENCE INTO A WEAKNESS, THENCE TO A LIGHTNESS, AND, BY THIS DECLENSION, INTO THE MADNESS WHEREIN NOW HE RAVES, AND ALL WE MOURN FOR.
DO YOU THINK 'TIS THIS?
HMMM...

HATH THERE BEEN SUCH A TIME, I'D FAIN KNOW THAT, THAT I HAVE POSITIVELY SAID 'TIS SO,' WHEN IT PROVED OTHERWISE?
IT MAY BE, VERY LIKELY.

NOT THAT I KNOW.

TAKE THIS FROM THIS, IF THIS BE OTHERWISE.
IF CIRCUMSTANCES LEAD ME, I WILL FIND WHERE TRUTH IS HID, THOUGH IT WERE HID INDEED WITHIN THE CENTRE.

HOW MAY WE TRY IT FURTHER?
YOU KNOW, SOMETIMES HE WALKS FOUR HOURS TOGETHER HERE IN THE LOBBY.
SO HE DOES INDEED.
AT SUCH A TIME I'LL LOOSE MY DAUGHTER TO HIM:
BE YOU AND I BEHIND AN ARRAS THEN; MARK THE ENCOUNTER:
IF HE LOVE HER NOT AND BE NOT FROM HIS REASON FALL'N THEREON, LET ME BE NO ASSISTANT FOR A STATE, BUT KEEP A FARM AND CARTERS.

WE WILL TRY IT.
OH!
BUT LOOK WHERE SADLY THE POOR WRETCH COMES READING.
AWAY, I DO BESEECH YOU, BOTH AWAY: I'LL BOARD HIM PRESENTLY.

O, GIVE ME LEAVE.

EXCELLENT WELL; YOU ARE A FISHMONGER.

NOT I, MY LORD.

EHEH...

HONEST, MY LORD!

THEN I WOULD YOU WERE SO HONEST A MAN.

FWUMP

AY, SIR; TO BE HONEST, AS THIS WORLD GOES, IS TO BE ONE MAN PICKED OUT OF TEN THOUSAND.

THAT'S VERY TRUE, MY LORD.

HOP

HOP

HOP~!

THWAP!
SHUF
FOR IF THE SUN BREED MAGGOTS IN A DEAD DOG, BEING A GOD KISSING CARRION -
HAVE YOU A DAUGHTER?

WHUMP

I HAVE, MY LORD.

LET HER NOT WALK I' THE SUN:
CONCEPTION IS A BLESSING: BUT NOT AS YOUR DAUGHTER MAY CONCEIVE. FRIEND, LOOK TO 'T.
HOW SAY YOU BY THAT?
STILL HARPING ON MY DAUGHTER: YET HE KNEW ME NOT AT FIRST; HE SAID I WAS A FISHMONGER: HE IS FAR GONE, FAR GONE:
AND TRULY IN MY YOUTH I SUFFERED MUCH EXTREMITY FOR LOVE; VERY NEAR THIS.
I'LL SPEAK TO HIM AGAIN.
WHAT DO YOU READ, MY LORD?

WORDS,
WORDS,
WORDS.
WHAT IS THE MATTER, MY LORD?
BETWEEN WHO?
I MEAN, THE MATTER THAT YOU READ, MY LORD.
SLANDERS, SIR:

FOR THE SATIRICAL ROGUE SAYS HERE THAT OLD MEN HAVE GREY BEARDS, THAT THEIR FACES ARE WRINKLED, THEIR EYES PURGING THICK AMBER AND PLUM-TREE GUM AND THAT THEY HAVE A PLENTIFUL LACK OF WIT, TOGETHER WITH MOST WEAK HAMS:
ALL WHICH, SIR, THOUGH I MOST POWERFULLY AND POTENTLY BELIEVE, YET I HOLD IT NOT HONESTY TO HAVE IT THUS SET DOWN,
FOR YOURSELF, SIR, SHOULD BE OLD AS I AM,
HOP
HOP
IF LIKE A CRAB YOU COULD GO BACKWARD.
THOUGH THIS BE MADNESS, YET THERE IS METHOD IN 'T.

WILL YOU WALK OUT OF THE AIR, MY LORD?
FWOMP
INTO MY GRAVE.
PHWOOO~
FLIT
INDEED, THAT IS OUT O' THE AIR.
HOW PREGNANT SOMETIMES HIS REPLIES ARE!

A HAPPINESS THAT OFTEN MADNESS HITS ON, WHICH REASON AND SANITY COULD NOT SO PROSPEROUSLY BE DELIVERED OF.

I WILL LEAVE HIM, AND SUDDENLY CONTRIVE THE MEANS OF MEETING BETWEEN HIM AND MY DAUGHTER.

MY HONOURABLE LORD, I WILL MOST HUMBLY TAKE MY LEAVE OF YOU.

WHAP!

YOU CANNOT, SIR, TAKE FROM ME ANYTHING THAT I WILL MORE WILLINGLY PART WITHAL:

EXCEPT MY LIFE.

FARE YOU WELL, MY LORD.

THP

TMP TMP

THESE TEDIOUS OLD FOOLS!

YOU GO TO SEEK THE LORD HAMLET; THERE HE IS.

OH!

AH!

MY EXCELLENT GOOD FRIENDS!
HOW DOST THOU, GUILDENSTERN? AH, ROSENCRANTZ!
GOOD LADS, HOW DO YE BOTH?
AS THE INDIFFERENT CHILDREN OF THE EARTH.
HAPPY, IN THAT WE ARE NOT OVER-HAPPY; ON FORTUNE'S CAP WE ARE NOT THE VERY BUTTON.
NOR THE SOLES OF HER SHOE?
NEITHER, MY LORD.

HEE HEE
THEN YOU LIVE ABOUT HER WAIST,
OR IN THE MIDDLE OF HER FAVOURS?
'FAITH, HER PRIVATES WE.
HA!
IN THE SECRET PARTS OF FORTUNE? O, MOST TRUE; SHE IS A STRUMPET.
WHAT'S THE NEWS?
NONE, MY LORD, BUT THAT THE WORLD'S GROWN HONEST.

THEN IS DOOMSDAY NEAR:

PRISON, MY LORD!
BUT YOUR NEWS IS NOT TRUE. LET ME QUESTION MORE IN PARTICULAR:
WHAT HAVE YOU, MY GOOD FRIENDS, DESERVED AT THE HANDS OF FORTUNE, THAT SHE SENDS YOU TO PRISON HITHER?

DENMARK'S A PRISON.

THEN IS THE WORLD ONE.

A GOODLY ONE; IN WHICH THERE ARE MANY CONFINES, WARDS AND DUNGEONS, DENMARK BEING ONE O' THE WORST.
WE THINK NOT SO, MY LORD.
WHY, THEN, 'TIS NONE TO YOU;
FOR THERE IS NOTHING EITHER GOOD OR BAD, BUT THINKING MAKES IT SO: TO ME IT IS A PRISON.
WHY THEN, YOUR AMBITION MAKES IT ONE; 'TIS TOO NARROW FOR YOUR MIND.

O GOD, I COULD BE BOUNDED IN A NUT SHELL AND COUNT MYSELF A KING OF INFINITE SPACE,
WERE IT NOT THAT I HAVE BAD DREAMS.
A DREAM ITSELF IS BUT A SHADOW.
WHICH DREAMS INDEED ARE AMBITION, FOR THE VERY SUBSTANCE OF THE AMBITIOUS IS MERELY THE SHADOW OF A DREAM.
TRULY, AND I HOLD AMBITION OF SO AIRY AND LIGHT A QUALITY THAT IT IS BUT A SHADOW'S SHADOW.

THEN ARE OUR BEGGARS BODIES, AND OUR MONARCHS AND OUTSTRETCHED HEROES THE BEGGARS' SHADOWS.
SHALL WE TO THE COURT? FOR, BY MY FAY, I CANNOT REASON.
WE'LL WAIT UPON YOU.
...
NO SUCH MATTER: I WILL NOT SORT YOU WITH THE REST OF MY SERVANTS, FOR, TO SPEAK TO YOU LIKE AN HONEST MAN, I AM MOST DREADFULLY ATTENDED.

TO VISIT YOU, MY LORD; NO OTHER OCCASION.
IN THE BEATEN WAY OF FRIENDSHIP, WHAT MAKE YOU AT ELSINORE?
BUT,
WERE YOU NOT SENT FOR? IS IT YOUR OWN INCLINING? IS IT A FREE VISITATION?
COME, DEAL JUSTLY WITH ME: COME, COME; NAY, SPEAK.
FWIP!
BEGGAR THAT I AM, I AM EVEN POOR IN THANKS; BUT I THANK YOU: AND SURE, DEAR FRIENDS, MY THANKS ARE TOO DEAR A HALFPENNY.
WHAT SHOULD WE SAY, MY LORD?

ERM...
WHY, ANY THING, BUT TO THE PURPOSE.
YOU WERE SENT FOR; AND THERE IS A KIND OF CONFESSION IN YOUR LOOKS WHICH YOUR MODESTIES HAVE NOT CRAFT ENOUGH TO COLOUR:
I KNOW THE GOOD KING AND QUEEN HAVE SENT FOR YOU.
TO WHAT END, MY LORD?
THAT YOU MUST TEACH ME.

BUT LET ME CONJURE YOU, BY THE RIGHTS OF OUR FELLOWSHIP, BY THE CONSONANCY OF OUR YOUTH, BY THE OBLIGATION OF OUR EVER-PRESERVED LOVE, AND BY WHAT MORE DEAR A BETTER PROPOSER COULD CHARGE YOU WITHAL, BE EVEN AND DIRECT WITH ME,
WHETHER YOU WERE SENT FOR, OR NO?
NAY, THEN, I HAVE AN EYE OF YOU -
WHAT SAY YOU?
IF YOU LOVE ME, HOLD NOT OFF.

MY LORD, WE WERE SENT FOR.
I WILL TELL YOU WHY; SO SHALL MY ANTICIPATION PREVENT YOUR DISCOVERY, AND YOUR SECRECY TO THE KING AND QUEEN MOULT NO FEATHER.
I HAVE OF LATE - BUT WHEREFORE I KNOW NOT - LOST ALL MY MIRTH, FORGONE ALL CUSTOM OF EXERCISES;
AND INDEED IT GOES SO HEAVILY WITH MY DISPOSITION THAT THIS GOODLY FRAME, THE EARTH, SEEMS TO ME A STERILE PROMONTORY,
THIS MOST EXCELLENT CANOPY, THE AIR, LOOK YOU, THIS BRAVE O'ERHANGING FIRMAMENT, THIS MAJESTICAL ROOF FRETTED WITH GOLDEN FIRE,
WHY, IT APPEARS NO OTHER THING TO ME THAN A FOUL AND PESTILENT CONGREGATION OF VAPOURS.

WHAT A PIECE OF WORK IS A MAN!
HOW NOBLE IN REASON!
HOW INFINITE IN FACULTY!
IN FORM AND MOVING HOW EXPRESS AND ADMIRABLE!
IN ACTION HOW LIKE AN ANGEL! IN APPREHENSION HOW LIKE A GOD!
THE BEAUTY OF THE WORLD! THE PARAGON OF ANIMALS!
AND YET, TO ME, WHAT IS THIS QUINTESSENCE OF DUST?

MAN DELIGHTS NOT ME: NO, NOR WOMAN NEITHER,
THOUGH BY YOUR SMILING YOU SEEM TO SAY SO.
MY LORD, THERE WAS NO SUCH STUFF IN MY THOUGHTS.
WHY DID YOU LAUGH THEN, WHEN I SAID 'MAN DELIGHTS NOT ME'?
TO THINK, MY LORD, IF YOU DELIGHT NOT IN MAN, WHAT LENTEN ENTERTAINMENT THE PLAYERS SHALL RECEIVE FROM YOU:
OH?

WE COTED THEM ON THE WAY; AND HITHER ARE THEY COMING, TO OFFER YOU SERVICE.
HE THAT PLAYS THE KING SHALL BE WELCOME; HIS MAJESTY SHALL HAVE TRIBUTE OF ME;
THE ADVENTUROUS KNIGHT SHALL USE HIS FOIL AND TARGET; THE LOVER SHALL NOT SIGH GRATIS; THE HUMOUROUS MAN SHALL END HIS PART IN PEACE;
THE CLOWN SHALL MAKE THOSE LAUGH WHOSE LUNGS ARE TICKLED O' THE SERE;
AND THE LADY SHALL SAY HER MIND FREELY, OR THE BLANK VERSE SHALL HALT FOR'T.
WHAT PLAYERS ARE THEY?
EVEN THOSE YOU WERE WONT TO TAKE DELIGHT IN, THE TRAGEDIANS OF THE CITY.
HOW CHANCES IT THEY TRAVEL? THEIR RESIDENCE, BOTH IN REPUTATION AND PROFIT, WAS BETTER BOTH WAYS.

I THINK THEIR INHIBITION COMES BY THE MEANS OF THE LATE INNOVATION.
DO THEY HOLD THE SAME ESTIMATION THEY DID WHEN I WAS IN THE CITY? ARE THEY SO FOLLOWED?
NO, INDEED, ARE THEY NOT.
HOW COMES IT? DO THEY GROW RUSTY?
NAY, THEIR ENDEAVOUR KEEPS IN THE WONTED PACE: BUT THERE IS, SIR, AN AERY OF CHILDREN, LITTLE EYASES, THAT CRY OUT ON THE TOP OF QUESTION, AND ARE MOST TYRANNICALLY CLAPPED FOR'T:
THESE ARE NOW THE FASHION, AND SO BERATTLE THE COMMON STAGES - SO THEY CALL THEM - THAT MANY WEARING RAPIERS ARE AFRAID OF GOOSE-QUILLS AND DARE SCARCE COME THITHER.

WHAT, ARE THEY CHILDREN? WHO MAINTAINS 'EM? HOW ARE THEY ESCOTED? WILL THEY PURSUE THE QUALITY NO LONGER THAN THEY CAN SING? WILL THEY NOT SAY AFTERWARDS,
IF THEY SHOULD GROW THEMSELVES TO COMMON PLAYERS - AS IT IS MOST LIKE, IF THEIR MEANS ARE NO BETTER - THEIR WRITERS DO THEM WRONG, TO MAKE THEM EXCLAIM AGAINST THEIR OWN SUCCESSION?
'FAITH, THERE HAS BEEN MUCH TO DO ON BOTH SIDES; AND THE NATION HOLDS IT NO SIN TO TARRE THEM TO CONTROVERSY:
THERE WAS, FOR A WHILE, NO MONEY BID FOR ARGUMENT, UNLESS THE POET AND THE PLAYER WENT TO CUFFS IN THE QUESTION.
IS'T POSSIBLE?

DO THE BOYS CARRY IT AWAY?
O, THERE HAS BEEN MUCH THROWING ABOUT OF BRAINS.
AY, THAT THEY DO, MY LORD; HERCULES AND HIS LOAD TOO.
IT IS NOT VERY STRANGE; FOR MINE UNCLE IS KING OF DENMARK,

AND THOSE THAT WOULD MAKE MOUTHS AT HIM WHILE MY FATHER LIVED, GIVE TWENTY, FORTY, FIFTY, AN HUNDRED DUCATS A-PIECE FOR HIS PICTURE IN LITTLE.
CLAT
CLATTER
'SBLOOD, THERE IS SOMETHING IN THIS MORE THAN NATURAL, IF PHILOSOPHY COULD FIND IT OUT.
!
THERE ARE THE PLAYERS.
GENTLEMEN, YOU ARE WELCOME TO ELSINORE. YOUR HANDS, COME THEN:

?

YOU ARE WELCOME:

THE APPURTENANCE OF WELCOME IS FASHION AND CEREMONY: LET ME COMPLY WITH YOU IN THIS GARB, LEST MY EXTENT TO THE PLAYERS, WHICH, I TELL YOU, MUST SHOW FAIRLY OUTWARD, SHOULD MORE APPEAR LIKE ENTERTAINMENT THAN YOURS.

IN WHAT, MY DEAR LORD?

BUT MY UNCLE-FATHER AND AUNT-MOTHER ARE DECEIVED.

I AM BUT MAD NORTH-NORTH-WEST:

SCRAW!
WHEN THE WIND IS SOUTHERLY I KNOW A HAWK FROM A HANDSAW.

WELL BE WITH YOU, GENTLEMEN!

? ? ?

HARK YOU, GUILDENSTERN, AND YOU TOO, AT EACH EAR A HEARER.

HAPPILY HE'S THE SECOND TIME COME TO THEM; FOR THEY SAY AN OLD MAN IS TWICE A CHILD.
HEH!
THAT GREAT BABY YOU SEE THERE IS NOT YET OUT OF HIS SWADDLING-CLOUTS.

I WILL PROPHESY HE COMES TO TELL ME OF THE PLAYERS; MARK IT.

MY LORD, I HAVE NEWS TO TELL YOU.

YOU SAY RIGHT, SIR: O' MONDAY MORNING; 'TWAS SO INDEED.
MY LORD, I HAVE NEWS TO TELL YOU.

WHEN ROSCIUS WAS AN ACTOR IN ROME -
THE ACTORS ARE COME HITHER, MY LORD.

UPON MINE HONOUR -
BUZ, BUZ!

THEN CAME EACH ACTOR ON HIS ASS -
THE BEST ACTORS IN THE WORLD, EITHER FOR TRAGEDY, COMEDY, HISTORY, PASTORAL, PASTORAL-COMICAL, HISTORICAL-PASTORAL, TRAGICAL-HISTORICAL, TRAGICAL-COMICAL-HISTORICAL-PASTORAL, SCENE INDIVIDABLE, OR POEM UNLIMITED: SENECA CANNOT BE TOO HEAVY, NOR PLAUTUS TOO LIGHT.
FOR THE LAW OF WRIT AND THE LIBERTY, THESE ARE THE ONLY MEN.
O JEPHTHAH, JUDGE OF ISRAEL, WHAT A TREASURE HADST THOU!
WHAT A TREASURE HAD HE, MY LORD?

'ONE FAIR DAUGHTER AND NO MORE, THE WHICH HE LOVED PASSING WELL.'
WHY,
STILL ON MY DAUGHTER.
NAY, THAT FOLLOWS NOT.
WHAT FOLLOWS, THEN, MY LORD?
AM I NOT I' THE RIGHT, OLD JEPHTHAH?
EHH?
WHY,
IF YOU CALL ME JEPHTHAH, MY LORD, I HAVE A DAUGHTER THAT I LOVE PASSING WELL.

'AS BY LOT,
GOD WOT,'

'IT CAME TO PASS, AS MOST LIKE IT WAS,' -

AND THEN, YOU KNOW,

THE FIRST ROW OF THE PIOUS CHANSON WILL SHOW YOU MORE;

FOR LOOK, WHERE MY ABRIDGEMENT COMES.

YOU ARE WELCOME, MASTERS; WELCOME, ALL.
I AM GLAD TO SEE THEE WELL.
WELCOME, GOOD FRIENDS.
O, MY OLD FRIEND! THY FACE IS VALENCED SINCE I SAW THEE LAST:
COMEST THOU TO BEARD ME IN DENMARK?

MASTERS, YOU ARE ALL WELCOME. WE'LL E'EN TO'T LIKE FRENCH FALCONERS, FLY AT ANY THING WE SEE:
WE'LL HAVE A SPEECH STRAIGHT: COME, GIVE US A TASTE OF YOUR QUALITY; COME, A PASSIONATE SPEECH.
WHAT, MY YOUNG LADY AND MISTRESS! BY'R LADY, YOUR LADYSHIP IS NEARER TO HEAVEN THAN WHEN I SAW YOU LAST, BY THE ALTITUDE OF A CHOPINE.
PRAY GOD, YOUR VOICE, LIKE APIECE OF UNCURRENT GOLD, BE NOT CRACKED WITHIN THE RING.
WHAT SPEECH, MY LORD?
I HEARD THEE SPEAK ME A SPEECH ONCE, BUT IT WAS NEVER ACTED; OR, IF IT WAS, NOT ABOVE ONCE; FOR THE PLAY, I REMEMBER, PLEASED NOT THE MILLION; 'TWAS CAVIARE TO THE GENERAL:
BUT IT WAS - AS I RECEIVED IT, AND OTHERS, WHOSE JUDGMENTS IN SUCH MATTERS CRIED IN THE TOP OF MINE - AN EXCELLENT PLAY, WELL DIGESTED IN THE SCENES, SET DOWN WITH AS MUCH MODESTY AS CUNNING.

I REMEMBER, ONE SAID THERE WERE NO SALLETS IN THE LINES TO MAKE THE MATTER SAVOURY, NOR NO MATTER IN THE PHRASE THAT MIGHT INDICT THE AUTHOR OF AFFECTATION;
BUT CALLED IT AN HONEST METHOD, AS WHOLESOME AS SWEET, AND BY VERY MUCH MORE HANDSOME THAN FINE.
LET ME SEE, LET ME SEE -
ONE SPEECH IN IT I CHIEFLY LOVED. 'TWAS AENEAS' TALE TO DIDO, AND THEREABOUT OF IT ESPECIALLY, WHERE HE SPEAKS OF PRIAM'S SLAUGHTER. IF IT LIVE IN YOUR MEMORY, BEGIN AT THIS LINE -
!

'THE RUGGED PYRRHUS, LIKE THE HYRCANIAN BEAST' -
IT IS NOT SO: IT BEGINS WITH PYRRHUS -
'THE RUGGED PYRRHUS, HE WHOSE SABLE ARMS, BLACK AS HIS PURPOSE, DID THE NIGHT RESEMBLE WHEN HE LAY COUCHED IN THE OMINOUS HORSE, HATH NOW THIS DREAD AND BLACK COMPLEXION SMEAR'D WITH HERALDRY MORE DISMAL;
HEAD TO FOOT NOW IS HE TOTAL GULES; HORRIDLY TRICK'D WITH BLOOD OF FATHERS, MOTHERS, DAUGHTERS, SONS,
BAKED AND IMPASTED WITH THE PARCHING STREETS, THAT LEND A TYRANNOUS AND DAMNED LIGHT TO THEIR LORD'S MURDER:

ROASTED IN WRATH AND FIRE, AND THUS O'ER-SIZED WITH COAGULATE GORE,
SO, PROCEED YOU.
WITH EYES LIKE CARBUNCLES, THE HELLISH PYRRHUS OLD GRANDSIRE PRIAM SEEKS.'
'FORE GOD, MY LORD, WELL SPOKEN, WITH GOOD ACCENT AND GOOD DISCRETION.
'ANON HE FINDS HIM STRIKING TOO SHORT AT GREEKS;
HIS ANTIQUE SWORD, REBELLIOUS TO HIS ARM, LIES WHERE IT FALLS, REPUGNANT TO COMMAND:
UNEQUAL MATCH'D, PYRRHUS AT PRIAM DRIVES; IN RAGE STRIKES WIDE; BUT WITH THE WHIFF AND WIND OF HIS FELL SWORD THE UNNERVED FATHER FALLS.
THEN SENSELESS ILIUM, SEEMING TO FEEL THIS BLOW, WITH FLAMING TOP STOOPS TO HIS BASE, AND WITH A HIDEOUS CRASH TAKES PRISONER PYRRHUS' EAR:

FOR, LO! HIS SWORD, WHICH WAS DECLINING ON THE MILKY HEAD OF REVEREND PRIAM, SEEM'D I' THE AIR TO STICK: SO, AS A PAINTED TYRANT, PYRRHUS STOOD, AND LIKE A NEUTRAL TO HIS WILL AND MATTER, DID NOTHING.

BUT, AS WE OFTEN SEE, AGAINST SOME STORM, A SILENCE IN THE HEAVENS, THE RACK STAND STILL, THE BOLD WINDS SPEECHLESS AND THE ORB BELOW AS HUSH AS DEATH, ANON THE DREADFUL THUNDER DOTH REND THE REGION, SO, AFTER PYRRHUS' PAUSE,

AROUSED VENGEANCE SETS HIM NEW A-WORK;

AND NEVER DID THE CYCLOPS' HAMMERS FALL ON MARS'S ARMOUR FORGED FOR PROOF ETERNE WITH LESS REMORSE THAN PYRRHUS' BLEEDING SWORD NOW FALLS ON PRIAM.

OUT, OUT, THOU STRUMPET, FORTUNE!
ALL YOU GODS, IN GENERAL SYNOD TAKE AWAY HER POWER; BREAK ALL THE SPOKES AND FELLIES FROM HER WHEEL, AND BOWL THE ROUND NAVE DOWN THE HILL OF HEAVEN, AS LOW AS TO THE FIENDS!'
...
HO-HUM
THIS IS TOO LONG.
IT SHALL TO THE BARBER'S, WITH YOUR BEARD.
PRITHEE, SAY ON:
HE'S FOR A JIG OR A TALE OF BAWDRY, OR HE SLEEPS:

SAY ON: COME TO HECUBA.
'BUT WHO, O, WHO HAD SEEN THE MOBLED QUEEN - '
'THE MOBLED QUEEN?'
THAT'S GOOD; 'MOBLED QUEEN' IS GOOD.
'RUN BAREFOOT UP AND DOWN, THREATENING THE FLAMES WITH BISSON RHEUM; A CLOUT UPON THAT HEAD WHERE LATE THE DIADEM STOOD, AND FOR A ROBE, ABOUT HER LANK AND ALL O'ER-TEEMED LOINS,
A BLANKET, IN THE ALARM OF FEAR CAUGHT UP; WHO THIS HAD SEEN, WITH TONGUE IN VENOM STEEP'D, 'GAINST FORTUNE'S STATE WOULD TREASON HAVE PRONOUNCED:

BUT IF THE GODS THEMSELVES DID SEE HER THEN WHEN SHE SAW PYRRHUS MAKE MALICIOUS SPORT IN MINCING WITH HIS SWORD HER HUSBAND'S LIMBS, THE INSTANT BURST OF CLAMOUR THAT SHE MADE,
UNLESS THINGS MORTAL MOVE THEM NOT AT ALL, WOULD HAVE MADE MILCH THE BURNING EYES OF HEAVEN, AND PASSION IN THE GODS.'
LOOK, WHETHER HE HAS NOT TURNED HIS COLOUR AND HAS TEARS IN'S EYES. PRAY YOU, NO MORE.
SNIF

GOOD MY LORD, WILL YOU SEE THE PLAYERS WELL BESTOWED? DO YOU HEAR, LET THEM BE WELL USED; FOR THEY ARE THE ABSTRACT AND BRIEF CHRONICLES OF THE TIME:

'TIS WELL: I'LL HAVE THEE SPEAK OUT THE REST SOON.

AFTER YOUR DEATH YOU WERE BETTER HAVE A BAD EPITAPH THAN THEIR ILL REPORT WHILE YOU LIVE.

GOD'S BODIKIN, MAN, MUCH BETTER:

MY LORD, I WILL USE THEM ACCORDING TO THEIR DESERT.

USE EVERY MAN AFTER HIS DESERT, AND WHO SHOULD 'SCAPE WHIPPING? USE THEM AFTER YOUR OWN HONOUR AND DIGNITY:
THE LESS THEY DESERVE, THE MORE MERIT IS IN YOUR BOUNTY.
TAKE THEM IN.
DOST THOU HEAR ME, OLD FRIEND; CAN YOU PLAY THE MURDER OF GONZAGO?
AY, MY LORD.
COME, SIRS.
FOLLOW HIM, FRIENDS: WE'LL HEAR A PLAY TO-MORROW.

AY, MY LORD.
WE'LL HA'T TO-MORROW NIGHT. YOU COULD, FOR A NEED, STUDY A SPEECH OF SOME DOZEN OR SIXTEEN LINES, WHICH I WOULD SET DOWN AND INSERT IN'T, COULD YOU NOT?
VERY WELL. FOLLOW THAT LORD;
AND LOOK YOU MOCK HIM NOT.
PAT
PAT
MY GOOD FRIENDS, I'LL LEAVE YOU TILL NIGHT: YOU ARE WELCOME TO ELSINORE.
GOOD MY LORD!
AY, SO, GOD BE WI' YE;

NOW I AM ALONE.
O, WHAT A ROGUE AND PEASANT SLAVE AM I!
IS IT NOT MONSTROUS THAT THIS PLAYER HERE,
BUT IN A FICTION, IN A DREAM OF PASSION, COULD FORCE HIS SOUL SO TO HIS OWN CONCEIT THAT FROM HER WORKING ALL HIS VISAGE WANN'D, TEARS IN HIS EYES, DISTRACTION IN'S ASPECT, A BROKEN VOICE, AND HIS WHOLE FUNCTION SUITING WITH FORMS TO HIS CONCEIT?
AND ALL FOR NOTHING!
FOR HECUBA!
WHAT'S HECUBA TO HIM, OR HE TO HECUBA, THAT HE SHOULD WEEP FOR HER? WHAT WOULD HE DO, HAD HE THE MOTIVE AND THE CUE FOR PASSION THAT I HAVE?
CLENCH
HE WOULD DROWN THE STAGE WITH TEARS AND CLEAVE THE GENERAL EAR WITH HORRID SPEECH, MAKE MAD THE GUILTY AND APPAL THE FREE, CONFOUND THE IGNORANT, AND AMAZE INDEED THE VERY FACULTIES OF EYES AND EARS.

YET I, A DULL AND MUDDY-METTLED RASCAL, PEAK, LIKE JOHN-A-DREAMS, UNPREGNANT OF MY CAUSE, AND CAN SAY NOTHING; NO, NOT FOR A KING, UPON WHOSE PROPERTY AND MOST DEAR LIFE A DAMN'D DEFEAT WAS MADE.
AM I A COWARD? WHO CALLS ME VILLAIN? BREAKS MY PATE ACROSS? PLUCKS OFF MY BEARD, AND BLOWS IT IN MY FACE? TWEAKS ME BY THE NOSE? GIVES ME THE LIE I' THE THROAT, AS DEEP AS TO THE LUNGS? WHO DOES ME THIS?
HA! 'SWOUNDS, I SHOULD TAKE IT: FOR IT CANNOT BE BUT I AM PIGEON-LIVER'D AND LACK GALL TO MAKE OPPRESSION BITTER, OR ERE THIS I SHOULD HAVE FATTED ALL THE REGION KITES WITH THIS SLAVE'S OFFAL:

O, VENGEANCE!
BLOODY, BAWDY VILLAIN! REMORSELESS, TREACHEROUS, LECHEROUS, KINDLESS VILLAIN!
WHY, WHAT AN ASS AM I! THIS IS MOST BRAVE, THAT I, THE SON OF A DEAR FATHER MURDER'D, PROMPTED TO MY REVENGE BY HEAVEN AND HELL,
SMACK!
MUST, LIKE A WHORE, UNPACK MY HEART WITH WORDS, AND FALL A-CURSING, LIKE A VERY DRAB, A SCULLION!

SMACK!

FIE UPON'T! FOH!

ABOUT, MY BRAIN!

!

I HAVE HEARD THAT GUILTY CREATURES SITTING AT A PLAY HAVE BY THE VERY CUNNING OF THE SCENE BEEN STRUCK SO TO THE SOUL THAT PRESENTLY THEY HAVE PROCLAIM'D THEIR MALEFACTIONS;
FOR MURDER, THOUGH IT HAVE NO TONGUE, WILL SPEAK WITH MOST MIRACULOUS ORGAN.

I'LL HAVE THESE PLAYERS PLAY SOMETHING LIKE THE MURDER OF MY FATHER BEFORE MINE UNCLE:
I'LL OBSERVE HIS LOOKS; I'LL TENT HIM TO THE QUICK: IF HE BUT BLENCH, I KNOW MY COURSE.

THE SPIRIT THAT I HAVE SEEN MAY BE THE DEVIL, AND THE DEVIL HATH POWER TO ASSUME A PLEASING SHAPE,
YEA, AND PERHAPS OUT OF MY WEAKNESS AND MY MELANCHOLY, AS HE IS VERY POTENT WITH SUCH SPIRITS, ABUSES ME TO DAMN ME.
I'LL HAVE GROUNDS MORE RELATIVE THAN THIS. THE PLAY'S THE THING WHEREIN I'LL CATCH THE CONSCIENCE OF THE KING.

THE CASTLE
ACT III
SCENE I
AND CAN YOU, BY NO DRIFT OF CIRCUMSTANCE, GET FROM HIM WHY HE PUTS ON THIS CONFUSION,
GRATING SO HARSHLY ALL HIS DAYS OF QUIET WITH TURBULENT AND DANGEROUS LUNACY?

HE DOES CONFESS HE FEELS HIMSELF DISTRACTED, BUT FROM WHAT CAUSE HE WILL BY NO MEANS SPEAK.

NOR DO WE FIND HIM FORWARD TO BE SOUNDED, BUT, WITH A CRAFTY MADNESS, KEEPS ALOOF, WHEN WE WOULD BRING HIM ON TO SOME CONFESSION OF HIS TRUE STATE.

BUT WITH MUCH FORCING OF HIS DISPOSITION.
NIGGARD OF QUESTION, BUT, OF OUR DEMANDS, MOST FREE IN HIS REPLY.

DID HE RECEIVE YOU WELL?
MOST LIKE A GENTLE-MAN.

DID YOU ASSAY HIM? TO ANY PASTIME?

MADAM, IT SO FELL OUT, THAT CERTAIN PLAYERS WE O'ER-RAUGHT ON THE WAY:
OF THESE WE TOLD HIM, AND THERE DID SEEM IN HIM A KIND OF JOY TO HEAR OF IT.
THEY ARE ABOUT THE COURT, AND, AS I THINK, THEY HAVE ALREADY ORDER THIS NIGHT TO PLAY BEFORE HIM.

'TIS MOST TRUE; AND HE BESEECH'D ME TO ENTREAT YOUR MAJESTIES TO HEAR AND SEE THE MATTER.
WITH ALL MY HEART; AND IT DOTH MUCH CONTENT ME TO HEAR HIM SO INCLINED.

CLI-CLACK
GOOD GENTLEMEN, GIVE HIM A FURTHER EDGE, AND DRIVE HIS PURPOSE ON TO THESE DELIGHTS.
WE SHALL, MY LORD.
SWEET GERTRUDE, LEAVE US TOO,
FOR WE HAVE CLOSELY SENT FOR HAMLET HITHER, THAT HE, AS 'TWERE BY ACCIDENT, MAY HERE AFFRONT OPHELIA.
HER FATHER AND MYSELF, LAWFUL ESPIALS, WILL SO BESTOW OURSELVES THAT, SEEING, UNSEEN,
WE MAY OF THEIR ENCOUNTER FRANKLY JUDGE, AND GATHER BY HIM, AS HE IS BEHAVED, IF 'T BE THE AFFLICTION OF HIS LOVE OR NO THAT THUS HE SUFFERS FOR.
I SHALL OBEY YOU.

AND FOR YOUR PART, OPHELIA,
I DO WISH THAT YOUR GOOD BEAUTIES BE THE HAPPY CAUSE OF HAMLET'S WILDNESS:
SO SHALL I HOPE YOUR VIRTUES WILL BRING HIM TO HIS WONTED WAY AGAIN, TO BOTH YOUR HONOURS.
MADAM, I WISH IT MAY.

- GRACIOUS, SO PLEASE YOU, WE WILL BESTOW OURSELVES -

OPHELIA, WALK YOU HERE.

READ ON THIS BOOK, THAT SHOW OF SUCH AN EXERCISE MAY COLOUR YOUR LONELINESS. - WE ARE OFT TO BLAME IN THIS,

FLIP
'TIS TOO MUCH PROVED - THAT WITH DEVOTION'S VISAGE AND PIOUS ACTION WE DO SUGAR O'ER THE DEVIL HIMSELF.
O, 'TIS TOO TRUE! HOW SMART A LASH THAT SPEECH DOTH GIVE MY CONSCIENCE! THE HARLOT'S CHEEK, BEAUTIED WITH PLASTERING ART, IS NOT MORE UGLY TO THE THING THAT HELPS IT THAN IS MY DEED TO MY MOST PAINTED WORD: O HEAVY BURTHEN!

AH!

SHUF...

SHUF...

SHUF...

I HEAR HIM COMING. LET'S WITHDRAW, MY LORD.

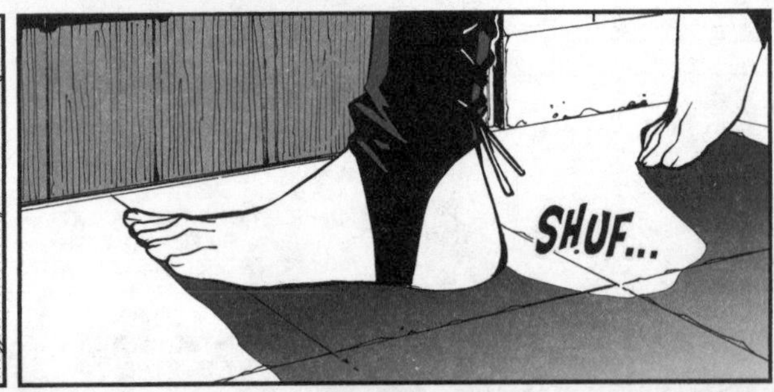

CLENCH
SHUF...
SHUF...
SHIIIIING

TO BE,
OR NOT TO BE,
THAT IS THE QUESTION.

WHETHER 'TIS NOBLER IN THE MIND TO SUFFER THE SLINGS AND ARROWS OF OUTRAGEOUS FORTUNE, OR TO TAKE ARMS AGAINST A SEA OF TROUBLES, AND BY OPPOSING END THEM?
TO DIE - TO SLEEP, NO MORE; AND BY A SLEEP TO SAY WE END THE HEART-ACHE AND THE THOUSAND NATURAL SHOCKS THAT FLESH IS HEIR TO; 'TIS A CONSUMMATION DEVOUTLY TO BE WISH'D.

TO DIE, TO SLEEP. TO SLEEP, PERCHANCE TO DREAM -
AY, THERE'S THE RUB; FOR IN THAT SLEEP OF DEATH WHAT DREAMS MAY COME WHEN WE HAVE SHUFFLED OFF THIS MORTAL COIL, MUST GIVE US PAUSE.
THERE'S THE RESPECT THAT MAKES CALAMITY OF SO LONG LIFE.

FOR WHO WOULD BEAR THE WHIPS AND SCORNS OF TIME,
THE OPPRESSOR'S WRONG,
THE PROUD MAN'S CONTUMELY,
THE PANGS OF DESPISED LOVE,
THE LAW'S DELAY,
THE INSOLENCE OF OFFICE AND...

THE SPURNS THAT PATIENT MERIT OF THE UNWORTHY TAKES, WHEN HE HIMSELF MIGHT HIS QUIETUS MAKE WITH A BARE BODKIN?
WHO WOULD THESE FARDELS BEAR, TO GRUNT AND SWEAT UNDER A WEARY LIFE, BUT THAT THE DREAD OF SOMETHING AFTER DEATH, THE UNDISCOVER'D COUNTRY FROM WHOSE BOURN NO TRAVELLER RETURNS,
PUZZLES THE WILL, AND MAKES US RATHER BEAR THOSE ILLS WE HAVE THAN FLY TO OTHERS THAT WE KNOW NOT OF?

THUS CONSCIENCE DOES MAKE COWARDS OF US ALL; AND THUS THE NATIVE HUE OF RESOLUTION IS SICKLIED O'ER WITH THE PALE CAST OF THOUGHT,
AND ENTERPRISES OF GREAT PITH AND MOMENT WITH THIS REGARD THEIR CURRENTS TURN AWRY, AND LOSE THE NAME OF ACTION.
...
STEP

SOFT YOU NOW!
THE FAIR OPHELIA! NYMPH, IN THY ORISONS BE ALL MY SINS REMEMBER'D.

GOOD MY LORD, HOW DOES YOUR HONOUR FOR THIS MANY A DAY?

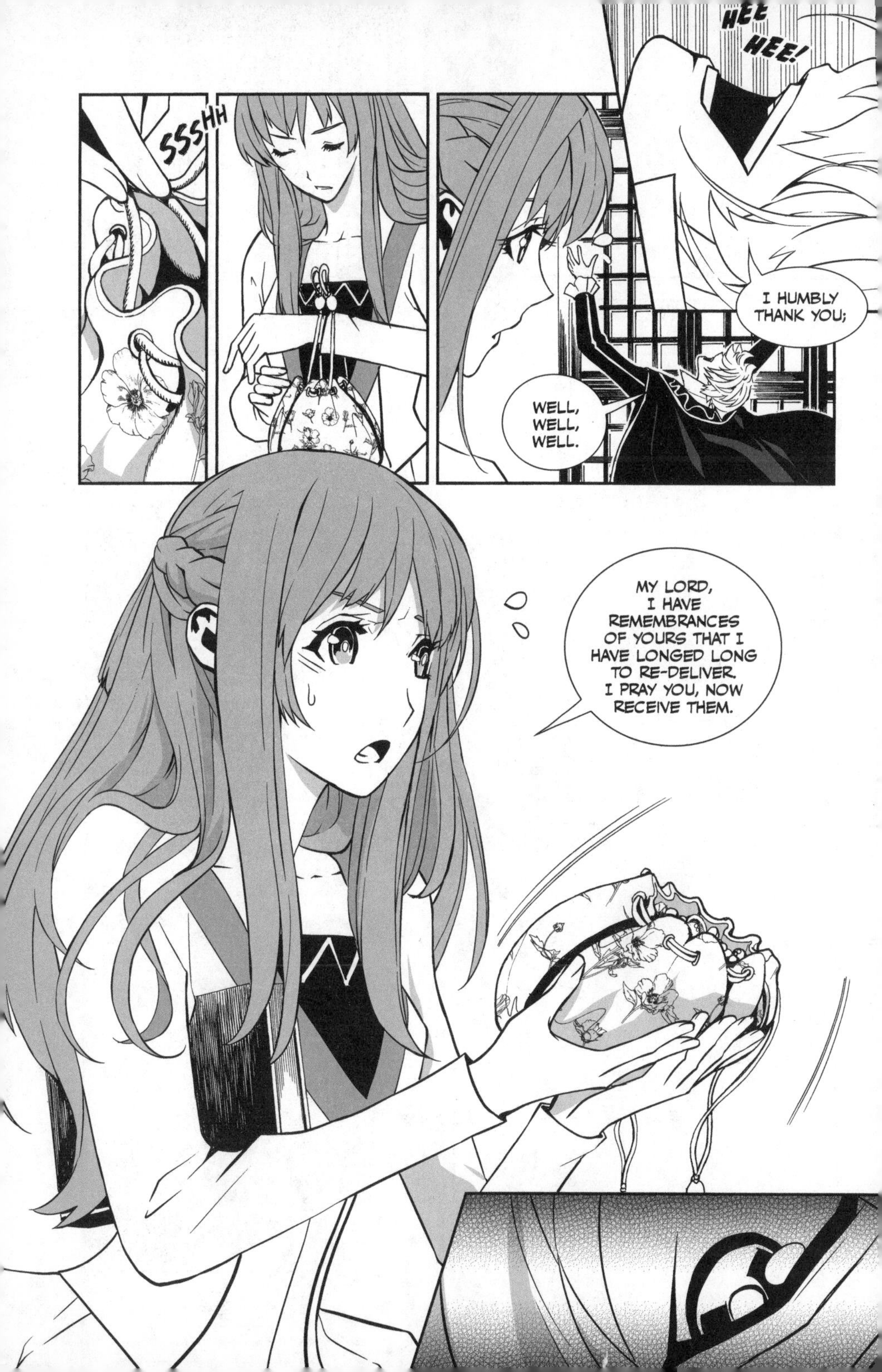
HEE HEE!
I HUMBLY THANK YOU;
WELL, WELL, WELL.
SSSHH
MY LORD, I HAVE REMEMBRANCES OF YOURS THAT I HAVE LONGED LONG TO RE-DELIVER. I PRAY YOU, NOW RECEIVE THEM.

NO, NOT I.
I NEVER GAVE YOU AUGHT.
MY HONOUR'D LORD, YOU KNOW RIGHT WELL YOU DID,
THEIR PERFUME LOST, TAKE THESE AGAIN;
AND, WITH THEM, WORDS OF SO SWEET BREATH COMPOSED AS MADE THE THINGS MORE RICH;

FOR TO THE NOBLE MIND RICH GIFTS WAX POOR WHEN GIVERS PROVE UNKIND.
THERE, MY LORD.
HA, HA! ARE YOU HONEST?
MY LORD?
ARE YOU FAIR?
WHAT MEANS YOUR LORDSHIP?

THAT IF YOU BE HONEST AND FAIR, YOUR HONESTY SHOULD ADMIT NO DISCOURSE TO YOUR BEAUTY.
AY, TRULY;
COULD BEAUTY, MY LORD, HAVE BETTER COMMERCE THAN WITH HONESTY?
FOR THE POWER OF BEAUTY WILL SOONER TRANSFORM HONESTY FROM WHAT IT IS TO A BAWD THAN THE FORCE OF HONESTY CAN TRANSLATE BEAUTY INTO HIS LIKENESS.
THIS WAS SOMETIME A PARADOX, BUT NOW THE TIME GIVES IT PROOF.

INDEED, MY LORD, YOU MADE ME BELIEVE SO.
I DID LOVE YOU ONCE.
FOR VIRTUE CANNOT SO INOCULATE OUR OLD STOCK BUT WE SHALL RELISH OF IT.
YOU SHOULD NOT HAVE BELIEVED ME;
I WAS THE MORE DECEIVED.
I LOVED YOU NOT.

GET THEE TO A NUNNERY. WHY WOULDST THOU BE A BREEDER OF SINNERS?
HA HA!
I AM MYSELF INDIFFERENT HONEST;
I AM VERY PROUD, REVENGEFUL, AMBITIOUS, WITH MORE OFFENCES AT MY BECK THAN I HAVE THOUGHTS TO PUT THEM IN, IMAGINATION TO GIVE THEM SHAPE, OR TIME TO ACT THEM IN.
WHAT SHOULD SUCH FELLOWS AS I DO CRAWLING BETWEEN EARTH AND HEAVEN?
WE ARE ARRANT KNAVES, ALL; BELIEVE NONE OF US.
BUT YET I COULD ACCUSE ME OF SUCH THINGS THAT
IT WERE BETTER MY MOTHER HAD NOT BORNE ME.

CREEEAK...

GO THY WAYS TO A NUNNERY.

...!

WHERE'S YOUR FATHER?

AT HOME, MY LORD.
LET THE DOORS BE SHUT UPON HIM, THAT HE MAY PLAY THE FOOL NOWHERE BUT IN'S OWN HOUSE.
FAREWELL.

O, HELP HIM, YOU SWEET HEAVENS!

IF THOU DOST MARRY, I'LL GIVE THEE THIS PLAGUE FOR THY DOWRY. BE THOU AS CHASTE AS ICE, AS PURE AS SNOW, THOU SHALT NOT ESCAPE CALUMNY.
GET THEE TO A NUNNERY, GO: FAREWELL.
OR, IF THOU WILT NEEDS MARRY, MARRY A FOOL; FOR WISE MEN KNOW WELL ENOUGH WHAT MONSTERS YOU MAKE OF THEM.
TO A NUNNERY, GO, AND QUICKLY TOO. FAREWELL.
O HEAVENLY POWERS, RESTORE HIM!
YOU JIG, YOU AMBLE, AND YOU LISP, AND NICKNAME GOD'S CREATURES, AND MAKE YOUR WANTONNESS YOUR IGNORANCE. GO TO, I'LL NO MORE ON'T; IT HATH MADE ME MAD.
SMAK!
GEEEEN~
I HAVE HEARD OF YOUR PAINTINGS TOO, WELL ENOUGH. GOD HAS GIVEN YOU ONE FACE, AND YOU MAKE YOURSELVES ANOTHER.

I SAY, WE WILL HAVE NO MORE MARRIAGES.
THOSE THAT ARE MARRIED ALREADY,
ALL BUT ONE, SHALL LIVE; THE REST SHALL KEEP AS THEY ARE.
TO A NUNNERY, GO.
SOB!
O, WHAT A NOBLE MIND IS HERE O'ERTHROWN!
THE COURTIER'S, SOLDIER'S, SCHOLAR'S, EYE, TONGUE, SWORD, THE EXPECTANCY AND ROSE OF THE FAIR STATE, THE GLASS OF FASHION AND THE MOULD OF FORM, THE OBSERVED OF ALL OBSERVERS, QUITE, QUITE DOWN!
AND I, OF LADIES MOST DEJECT AND WRETCHED, THAT SUCK'D THE HONEY OF HIS MUSIC VOWS, NOW SEE THAT NOBLE AND MOST SOVEREIGN REASON, LIKE SWEET BELLS JANGLED, OUT OF TUNE AND HARSH;
THAT UNMATCH'D FORM AND FEATURE OF BLOWN YOUTH BLASTED WITH ECSTASY.
O, WOE IS ME, TO HAVE SEEN WHAT I HAVE SEEN, SEE WHAT I SEE!

HIS AFFECTIONS DO NOT THAT WAY TEND,
NOR WHAT HE SPAKE, THOUGH IT LACK'D FORM A LITTLE, WAS NOT LIKE MADNESS.
SLAM!
AHUH HUH HUH...
LOVE?
WHAT THINK YOU ON'T?
THERE'S SOMETHING IN HIS SOUL, O'ER WHICH HIS MELANCHOLY SITS ON BROOD; AND I DO DOUBT THE HATCH AND THE DISCLOSE WILL BE SOME DANGER,
WHICH FOR TO PREVENT, I HAVE IN QUICK DETERMINATION THUS SET IT DOWN: HE SHALL WITH SPEED TO ENGLAND, FOR THE DEMAND OF OUR NEGLECTED TRIBUTE:
HAPLY THE SEAS AND COUNTRIES DIFFERENT, WITH VARIABLE OBJECTS, SHALL EXPEL THIS SOMETHING-SETTLED MATTER IN HIS HEART, WHEREON HIS BRAINS STILL BEATING PUTS HIM THUS FROM FASHION OF HIMSELF.
IT SHALL DO WELL. BUT YET DO I BELIEVE THE ORIGIN AND COMMENCEMENT OF HIS GRIEF SPRUNG FROM NEGLECTED LOVE.

MY LORD, DO AS YOU PLEASE;
HOW NOW, OPHELIA! YOU NEED NOT TELL US WHAT LORD HAMLET SAID; WE HEARD IT ALL.
BUT, IF YOU HOLD IT FIT, AFTER THE PLAY LET HIS QUEEN MOTHER ALL ALONE ENTREAT HIM TO SHOW HIS GRIEF,
LET HER BE ROUND WITH HIM; AND I'LL BE PLACED, SO PLEASE YOU, IN THE EAR OF ALL THEIR CONFERENCE.
IF SHE FIND HIM NOT, TO ENGLAND SEND HIM, OR CONFINE HIM WHERE YOUR WISDOM BEST SHALL THINK.

IT SHALL BE SO. MADNESS IN GREAT ONES MUST NOT UNWATCH'D GO.

ACT III
SCENE II
THE CASTLE

SPEAK THE SPEECH, I PRAY YOU, AS I PRONOUNCED IT TO YOU, TRIPPINGLY ON THE TONGUE:

NOR DO NOT SAW THE AIR TOO MUCH WITH YOUR HAND, THUS,

SAW SAW

BUT IF YOU MOUTH IT, AS MANY OF YOUR PLAYERS DO, I HAD AS LIEF THE TOWN-CRIER SPOKE MY LINES.

BUT USE ALL GENTLY; FOR IN THE VERY TORRENT, TEMPEST, AND, AS I MAY SAY, THE WHIRLWIND OF PASSION,

YOU MUST ACQUIRE AND BEGET A TEMPERANCE THAT MAY GIVE IT SMOOTHNESS.

O, IT OFFENDS ME TO THE SOUL
NYAGH!

TO HEAR A ROBUSTIOUS PERIWIG-PATED FELLOW TEAR A PASSION TO TATTERS, TO VERY RAGS, TO SPLIT THE EARS OF THE GROUNDLINGS,
WHO FOR THE MOST PART ARE CAPABLE OF NOTHING BUT INEXPLICABLE DUMBSHOWS AND NOISE.
I WOULD HAVE SUCH A FELLOW WHIPPED FOR O'ERDOING TERMAGANT. IT OUT-HERODS HEROD.
BE NOT TOO TAME NEITHER, BUT LET YOUR OWN DISCRETION BE YOUR TUTOR.
PRAY YOU, AVOID IT.
I WARRANT YOUR HONOUR.
SUIT THE ACTION TO THE WORD, THE WORD TO THE ACTION,
WITH THIS SPECIAL OBSERVANCE, THAT YOU O'ERSTEP NOT THE MODESTY OF NATURE; FOR ANY THING SO OVERDONE IS FROM THE PURPOSE OF PLAYING,

WHOSE END, BOTH AT THE FIRST AND NOW, WAS AND IS, TO HOLD, AS 'TWERE, THE MIRROR UP TO NATURE; TO SHOW VIRTUE HER OWN FEATURE, SCORN HER OWN IMAGE, AND THE VERY AGE AND BODY OF THE TIME HIS FORM AND PRESSURE.
NOW, THIS OVERDONE, OR COME TARDY OFF, THOUGH IT MAKE THE UNSKILFUL LAUGH, CANNOT BUT MAKE THE JUDICIOUS GRIEVE;
THE CENSURE OF THE WHICH ONE MUST IN YOUR ALLOWANCE O'ERWEIGH A WHOLE THEATRE OF OTHERS.
HUP!
O, THERE BE PLAYERS THAT I HAVE SEEN PLAY, AND HEARD OTHERS PRAISE, AND THAT HIGHLY,
NOT TO SPEAK IT PROFANELY, THAT, NEITHER HAVING THE ACCENT OF CHRISTIANS NOR THE GAIT OF CHRISTIAN, PAGAN, NOR MAN,
HAVE SO STRUTTED AND BELLOWED THAT I HAVE THOUGHT SOME OF NATURE'S JOURNEYMEN HAD MADE MEN AND NOT MADE THEM WELL, THEY IMITATED HUMANITY SO ABOMINABLY.
I HOPE WE HAVE REFORMED THAT INDIFFERENTLY WITH US, SIR.

O, REFORM IT ALTOGETHER.
AND LET THOSE THAT PLAY YOUR CLOWNS SPEAK NO MORE THAN IS SET DOWN FOR THEM,
FOR THERE BE OF THEM THAT WILL THEMSELVES LAUGH, TO SET ON SOME QUANTITY OF BARREN SPECTATORS TO LAUGH TOO; THOUGH, IN THE MEANTIME, SOME NECESSARY QUESTION OF THE PLAY BE THEN TO BE CONSIDERED.
THAT'S VILLAINOUS, AND SHOWS A MOST PITIFUL AMBITION IN THE FOOL THAT USES IT.
GO, MAKE YOU READY.
HOW NOW, MY LORD! WILL THE KING HEAR THIS PIECE OF WORK?
AND THE QUEEN TOO, AND THAT PRESENTLY.

WILL YOU TWO HELP TO HASTEN THEM?
WE WILL, MY LORD.

BID THE PLAYERS MAKE HASTE.

HERE, SWEET LORD, AT YOUR SERVICE.

WHAT HO! HORATIO!

UM...
HORATIO, THOU ART E'EN AS JUST A MAN AS E'ER MY CONVERSATION COPED WITHAL.
O, MY DEAR LORD -

NAY, DO NOT THINK I FLATTER; FOR WHAT ADVANCEMENT MAY I HOPE FROM THEE

THAT NO REVENUE HAST BUT THY GOOD SPIRITS, TO FEED AND CLOTHE THEE? WHY SHOULD THE POOR BE FLATTER'D?

NO, LET THE CANDIED TONGUE LICK ABSURD POMP, AND CROOK THE PREGNANT HINGES OF THE KNEE WHERE THRIFT MAY FOLLOW FAWNING. DOST THOU HEAR?

MURMUR

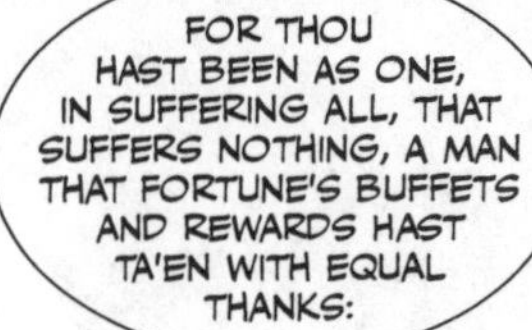

FOR THOU HAST BEEN AS ONE, IN SUFFERING ALL, THAT SUFFERS NOTHING, A MAN THAT FORTUNE'S BUFFETS AND REWARDS HAST TA'EN WITH EQUAL THANKS:

SINCE MY DEAR SOUL WAS MISTRESS OF HER CHOICE AND COULD OF MEN DISTINGUISH, HER ELECTION HATH SEAL'D THEE FOR HERSELF;
PAT

AND BLEST ARE THOSE WHOSE BLOOD AND JUDGMENT ARE SO WELL COMMINGLED, THAT THEY ARE NOT A PIPE FOR FORTUNE'S FINGER TO SOUND WHAT STOP SHE PLEASE.
GIVE ME THAT MAN THAT IS NOT PASSION'S SLAVE, AND I WILL WEAR HIM IN MY HEART'S CORE,
AY, IN MY HEART OF HEART, AS I DO THEE -
SOMETHING TOO MUCH OF THIS -
THERE IS A PLAY TO-NIGHT BEFORE THE KING; ONE SCENE OF IT COMES NEAR THE CIRCUMSTANCE WHICH I HAVE TOLD THEE OF MY FATHER'S DEATH:
I PRITHEE, WHEN THOU SEEST THAT ACT AFOOT, EVEN WITH THE VERY COMMENT OF THY SOUL OBSERVE MINE UNCLE: IF HIS OCCULTED GUILT DO NOT ITSELF UNKENNEL IN ONE SPEECH,
IT IS A DAMNED GHOST THAT WE HAVE SEEN, AND MY IMAGINATIONS ARE AS FOUL AS VULCAN'S STITHY.

WELL, MY LORD: IF HE STEAL AUGHT THE WHILST THIS PLAY IS PLAYING, AND 'SCAPE DETECTING, I WILL PAY THE THEFT.
GIVE HIM HEEDFUL NOTE; FOR I MINE EYES WILL RIVET TO HIS FACE, AND AFTER WE WILL BOTH OUR JUDGMENTS JOIN IN CENSURE OF HIS SEEMING.
THEY ARE COMING TO THE PLAY. I MUST BE IDLE. GET YOU A PLACE.
HOW FARES OUR COUSIN HAMLET?

EXCELLENT, I' FAITH; OF THE CHAMELEON'S DISH: I EAT THE AIR, PROMISE-CRAMMED: YOU CANNOT FEED CAPONS SO.
AGL AGL!
THESE WORDS ARE NOT MINE.
NO, NOR MINE NOW.
AGL.
I HAVE NOTHING WITH THIS ANSWER, HAMLET;
MY LORD, YOU PLAYED ONCE I' THE UNIVERSITY, YOU SAY?
THAT DID I, MY LORD; AND WAS ACCOUNTED A GOOD ACTOR.
WHAT DID YOU ENACT?

I DID ENACT JULIUS CAESAR. I WAS KILLED I' THE CAPITOL; BRUTUS KILLED ME.
IT WAS A BRUTE PART OF HIM TO KILL SO CAPITAL A CALF THERE.
BE THE PLAYERS READY?
ZWIP
AY, MY LORD; THEY STAY UPON YOUR PATIENCE.
COME HITHER,

MY DEAR HAMLET, SIT BY ME.
HERE'S METAL MORE ATTRACTIVE.
NO, GOOD MOTHER,
O, HO! DO YOU MARK THAT?
...
FWUMP!
LADY, SHALL I LIE IN YOUR LAP?
NO, MY LORD.

I MEAN, MY HEAD UPON YOUR LAP?
FWUMP!
AY, MY LORD.
DO YOU THINK I MEANT COUNTRY MATTERS?
I THINK NOTHING, MY LORD.
THAT'S A FAIR THOUGHT TO LIE BETWEEN MAIDS' LEGS.
RUB RUB
WHAT IS, MY LORD?

FOR, LOOK YOU, HOW CHEERFULLY MY MOTHER LOOKS, AND MY FATHER DIED WITHIN THESE TWO HOURS.
O GOD, YOUR ONLY JIG-MAKER! WHAT SHOULD A MAN DO BUT BE MERRY?

NAY, 'TIS TWICE TWO MONTHS, MY LORD.
SO LONG?

FWAP!
O HEAVENS! DIE TWO MONTHS AGO, AND NOT FORGOTTEN YET?
THEN THERE'S HOPE A GREAT MAN'S MEMORY MAY OUTLIVE HIS LIFE HALF A YEAR. BUT, BY'R LADY, HE MUST BUILD CHURCHES, THEN; OR ELSE SHALL HE SUFFER NOT THINKING ON, WITH THE HOBBY-HORSE, WHOSE EPITAPH IS 'FOR, O, FOR, O, THE HOBBY-HORSE IS FORGOT.'
NAY THEN, LET THE DEVIL WEAR BLACK, FOR I'LL HAVE A SUIT OF SABLES.

GASP!

TIP~
TIK!
DRIP
GAH-HURK!
SOB
SOB

BOW~
WHAT MEANS THIS, MY LORD?

MARRY, THIS IS MICHING MALLECHO;

IT MEANS MISCHIEF.

WILL HE TELL US WHAT THIS SHOW MEANT?

AY, OR ANY SHOW THAT YOU'LL SHOW HIM. BE NOT YOU ASHAMED TO SHOW, HE'LL NOT SHAME TO TELL YOU WHAT IT MEANS.

YOU ARE NAUGHT, YOU ARE NAUGHT: I'LL MARK THE PLAY.

FOR US, AND FOR OUR TRAGEDY, HERE STOOPING TO YOUR CLEMENCY, WE BEG YOUR HEARING PATIENTLY.

IS THIS A PROLOGUE, OR THE POSY OF A RING?

'TIS BRIEF, MY LORD.

AS WOMAN'S LOVE.

SINCE LOVE OUR HEARTS AND HYMEN DID OUR HANDS UNITE COMMUTUAL IN MOST SACRED BANDS.
FULL THIRTY TIMES HATH PHOEBUS' CART GONE ROUND NEPTUNE'S SALT WASH AND TELLUS' ORBED GROUND, AND THIRTY DOZEN MOONS WITH BORROW'D SHEEN ABOUT THE WORLD HAVE TIMES TWELVE THIRTIES BEEN,
SO MANY JOURNEYS MAY THE SUN AND MOON MAKE US AGAIN COUNT O'ER ERE LOVE BE DONE.
BUT WOE IS ME! YOU ARE SO SICK OF LATE, SO FAR FROM CHEER AND FROM YOUR FORMER STATE, THAT I DISTRUST YOU.
YET THOUGH I DISTRUST, DISCOMFORT YOU, MY LORD, IT NOTHING MUST. FOR WOMEN'S FEAR AND LOVE HOLDS QUANTITY, IN NEITHER AUGHT, OR IN EXTREMITY.
NOW WHAT MY LOVE IS, PROOF HATH MADE YOU KNOW, AND AS MY LOVE IS SIZED, MY FEAR IS SO: WHERE LOVE IS GREAT, THE LITTLEST DOUBTS ARE FEAR. WHERE LITTLE FEARS GROW GREAT, GREAT LOVE GROWS THERE.

FAITH, I MUST LEAVE THEE, LOVE, AND SHORTLY TOO.
MY OPERANT POWERS THEIR FUNCTIONS LEAVE TO DO. AND THOU SHALT LIVE IN THIS FAIR WORLD BEHIND, HONOUR'D, BELOVED, AND HAPLY ONE AS KIND FOR HUSBAND SHALT THOU -
O, CONFOUND THE REST! SUCH LOVE MUST NEEDS BE TREASON IN MY BREAST.
IN SECOND HUSBAND LET ME BE ACCURST!
NONE WED THE SECOND BUT WHO KILL'D THE FIRST.

WORMWOOD.

WORMWOOD,

THE INSTANCES THAT SECOND MARRIAGE MOVE ARE BASE RESPECTS OF THRIFT, BUT NONE OF LOVE.
A SECOND TIME I KILL MY HUSBAND DEAD, WHEN SECOND HUSBAND KISSES ME IN BED.

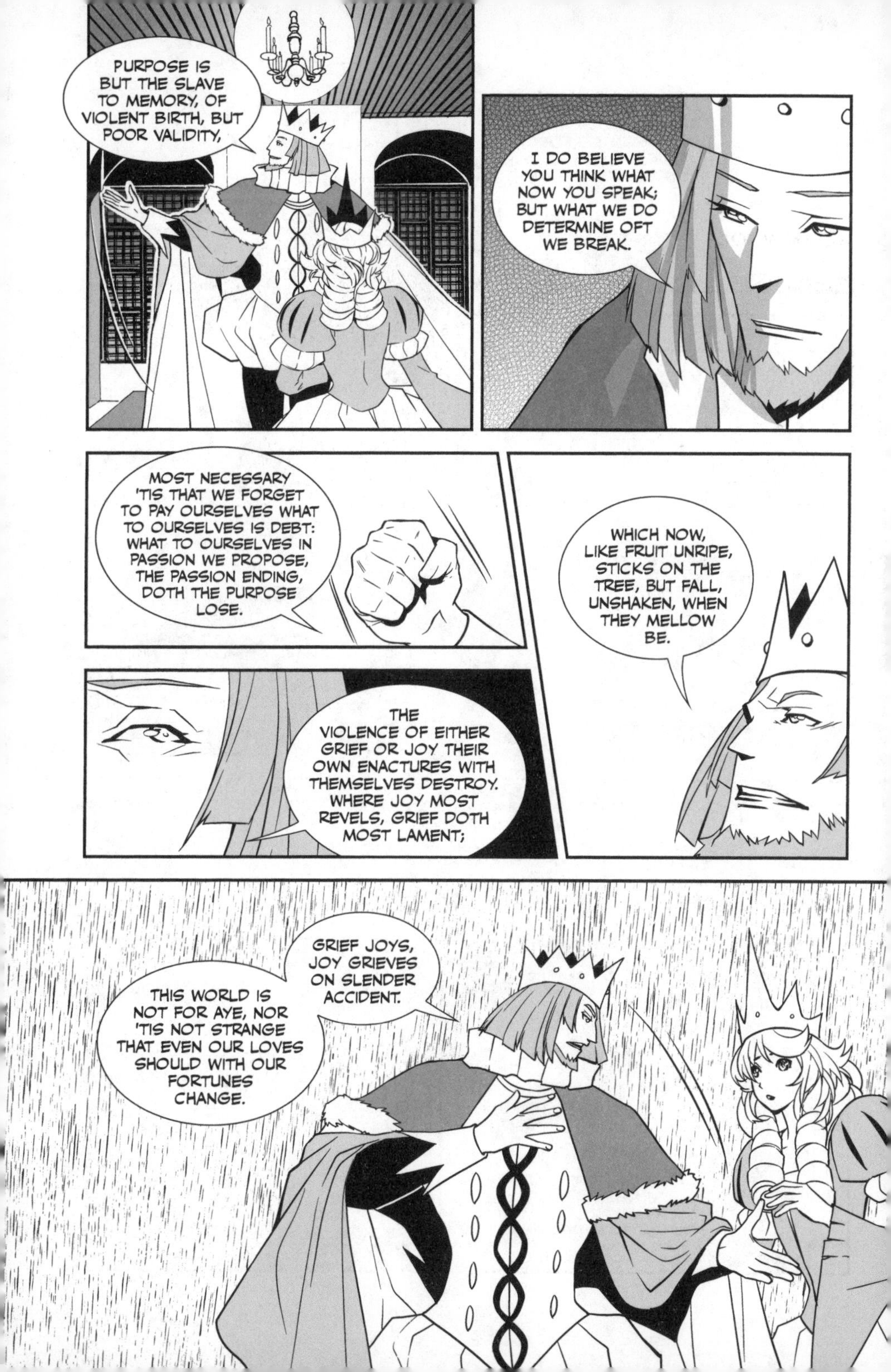

PURPOSE IS BUT THE SLAVE TO MEMORY, OF VIOLENT BIRTH, BUT POOR VALIDITY,
I DO BELIEVE YOU THINK WHAT NOW YOU SPEAK; BUT WHAT WE DO DETERMINE OFT WE BREAK.
MOST NECESSARY 'TIS THAT WE FORGET TO PAY OURSELVES WHAT TO OURSELVES IS DEBT: WHAT TO OURSELVES IN PASSION WE PROPOSE, THE PASSION ENDING, DOTH THE PURPOSE LOSE.
WHICH NOW, LIKE FRUIT UNRIPE, STICKS ON THE TREE, BUT FALL, UNSHAKEN, WHEN THEY MELLOW BE.
THE VIOLENCE OF EITHER GRIEF OR JOY THEIR OWN ENACTURES WITH THEMSELVES DESTROY. WHERE JOY MOST REVELS, GRIEF DOTH MOST LAMENT;
GRIEF JOYS, JOY GRIEVES ON SLENDER ACCIDENT.
THIS WORLD IS NOT FOR AYE, NOR 'TIS NOT STRANGE THAT EVEN OUR LOVES SHOULD WITH OUR FORTUNES CHANGE.

THE GREAT MAN DOWN, YOU MARK HIS FAVOURITE FLIES; THE POOR ADVANCED MAKES FRIENDS OF ENEMIES.
FOR 'TIS A QUESTION LEFT US YET TO PROVE, WHETHER LOVE LEAD FORTUNE, OR ELSE FORTUNE LOVE.
AND HITHERTO DOTH LOVE ON FORTUNE TEND,
FOR WHO NOT NEEDS SHALL NEVER LACK A FRIEND, AND WHO IN WANT A HOLLOW FRIEND DOTH TRY, DIRECTLY SEASONS HIM HIS ENEMY.
SO THINK THOU WILT NO SECOND HUSBAND WED, BUT DIE THY THOUGHTS WHEN THY FIRST LORD IS DEAD.
BUT, ORDERLY TO END WHERE I BEGUN, OUR WILLS AND FATES DO SO CONTRARY RUN THAT OUR DEVICES STILL ARE OVERTHROWN.
OUR THOUGHTS ARE OURS, THEIR ENDS NONE OF OUR OWN.

NOR EARTH TO ME GIVE FOOD, NOR HEAVEN LIGHT! SPORT AND REPOSE LOCK FROM ME DAY AND NIGHT!
TO DESPERATION TURN MY TRUST AND HOPE! AN ANCHOR'S CHEER IN PRISON BE MY SCOPE!
EACH OPPOSITE THAT BLANKS THE FACE OF JOY MEET WHAT I WOULD HAVE WELL AND IT DESTROY! BOTH HERE AND HENCE PURSUE ME LASTING STRIFE, IF, ONCE A WIDOW, EVER I BE WIFE!
IF SHE SHOULD BREAK IT NOW!
'TIS DEEPLY SWORN.

SLEEP ROCK THY BRAIN, AND NEVER COME MISCHANCE BETWEEN US TWAIN.

PECK~

SWEET, LEAVE ME HERE AWHILE.
MY SPIRITS GROW DULL, AND FAIN I WOULD BEGUILE THE TEDIOUS DAY WITH SLEEP.

MADAM, HOW LIKE YOU THIS PLAY?

FWUMP

THUMP

O, BUT SHE'LL KEEP HER WORD.

THE LADY PROTESTS TOO MUCH, METHINKS.

HAVE YOU HEARD THE ARGUMENT? IS THERE NO OFFENCE IN 'T?

POISON IN JEST. NO OFFENCE I' THE WORLD.

NO, NO, THEY DO BUT JEST.

WHAT DO YOU CALL THE PLAY?
THE MOUSE-TRAP.
GASP!
MARRY, HOW? TROPICALLY.
THIS PLAY IS THE IMAGE OF A MURDER DONE IN VIENNA. GONZAGO IS THE DUKE'S NAME, HIS WIFE BAPTISTA. YOU SHALL SEE ANON.
'TIS A KNAVISH PIECE OF WORK, BUT WHAT O' THAT?

YOUR MAJESTY AND WE THAT HAVE FREE SOULS, IT TOUCHES US NOT.
LET THE GALLED JADE WINCE, OUR WITHERS ARE UNWRUNG.
THIS IS ONE LUCIANUS, NEPHEW TO THE KING.
ZIP!
YOU ARE AS GOOD AS A CHORUS, MY LORD.
I COULD INTERPRET BETWEEN YOU AND YOUR LOVE, IF I COULD SEE THE PUPPETS DALLYING.

YOU ARE KEEN, MY LORD, YOU ARE KEEN.
IT WOULD COST YOU A GROANING TO TAKE OFF MY EDGE.
EEK!
STILL BETTER AND WORSE.
FWOMP
SO YOU MUST TAKE YOUR HUSBANDS.

BEGIN, MURDERER.
POX, LEAVE THY DAMNABLE FACES, AND BEGIN.
COME: 'THE CROAKING RAVEN DOTH BELLOW FOR REVENGE.'
THY NATURAL MAGIC AND DIRE PROPERTY ON WHOLESOME LIFE USURP IMMEDIATELY.
THOUGHTS BLACK, HANDS APT, DRUGS FIT, AND TIME AGREEING, CONFEDERATE SEASON, ELSE NO CREATURE SEEING,
THOU MIXTURE RANK, OF MIDNIGHT WEEDS COLLECTED, WITH HECATE'S BAN THRICE BLASTED, THRICE INFECTED,
DR-IP

AGGCK-!

HE POISONS HIM I' THE GARDEN FOR 'S ESTATE. HIS NAME'S GONZAGO.

THE STORY IS EXTANT, AND WRIT IN CHOICE ITALIAN.

YOU SHALL SEE ANON HOW THE MURDERER GETS THE LOVE OF GONZAGO'S WIFE.

GASP!

THE KING RISES.

WHAT, FRIGHTED WITH FALSE FIRE?

SHUF

GIVE O'ER THE PLAY.

HOW FARES MY LORD?

GIVE ME SOME LIGHT,

AWAY!

WHY, LET THE STRICKEN DEER GO WEEP, THE HART UNGALLED PLAY.

FOR SOME MUST WATCH, WHILE SOME MUST SLEEP. SO RUNS THE WORLD AWAY.

HYAA-!
WOULD NOT THIS, SIR, AND A FOREST OF FEATHERS - IF THE REST OF MY FORTUNES TURN TURK WITH ME - WITH TWO PROVINCIAL ROSES ON MY RAZED SHOES,
GET ME A FELLOWSHIP IN A CRY OF PLAYERS, SIR?
HALF A SHARE.
A WHOLE ONE, I.
THUD
FOR THOU DOST KNOW, O DAMON DEAR,
THIS REALM DISMANTLED WAS OF JOVE HIMSELF; AND NOW REIGNS HERE A VERY, VERY - PAJOCK.

O GOOD HORATIO, I'LL TAKE THE GHOST'S WORD FOR A THOUSAND POUND. DIDST PERCEIVE?
YOU MIGHT HAVE RHYMED.
VERY WELL, MY LORD.
UPON THE TALK OF THE POISONING?
I DID VERY WELL NOTE HIM.

FOR IF THE KING LIKE NOT THE COMEDY, WHY THEN, BELIKE, HE LIKES IT NOT, PERDY.

AH, HA! COME, SOME MUSIC! COME, THE RECORDERS!

HA-HA!
COME, SOME MUSIC!

THE KING, SIR -

AY, SIR, WHAT OF HIM?

IS IN HIS RETIREMENT MARVELOUS DISTEMPERED.

GOOD MY LORD, VOUCHSAFE ME A WORD WITH YOU.
SIR, A WHOLE HISTORY.

WITH DRINK, SIR?
FWUD
NO, MY LORD, RATHER WITH CHOLER.
YOUR WISDOM SHOULD SHOW ITSELF MORE RICHER TO SIGNIFY THIS TO HIS DOCTOR; FOR, FOR ME TO PUT HIM TO HIS PURGATION WOULD PERHAPS PLUNGE HIM INTO FAR MORE CHOLER.
GOOD MY LORD, PUT YOUR DISCOURSE INTO SOME FRAME AND START NOT SO WILDLY FROM MY AFFAIR.
I AM TAME, SIR. PRONOUNCE.
THE QUEEN YOUR MOTHER, IN MOST GREAT AFFLICTION OF SPIRIT, HATH SENT ME TO YOU.

IF IT SHALL PLEASE YOU TO MAKE ME A WHOLESOME ANSWER, I WILL DO YOUR MOTHER'S COMMANDMENT. IF NOT, YOUR PARDON AND MY RETURN SHALL BE THE END OF MY BUSINESS.

YOU ARE WELCOME.
NAY, GOOD MY LORD, THIS COURTESY IS NOT OF THE RIGHT BREED.

SIR, I CANNOT.

WHAT, MY LORD?

MAKE YOU A WHOLESOME ANSWER. MY WIT'S DISEASED. BUT, SIR, SUCH ANSWER AS I CAN MAKE, YOU SHALL COMMAND. OR, RATHER, AS YOU SAY, MY MOTHER. THEREFORE NO MORE BUT TO THE MATTER. MY MOTHER, YOU SAY -

O!
THEN THUS SHE SAYS: YOUR BEHAVIOR HATH STRUCK HER INTO AMAZEMENT AND ADMIRATION.
WONDERFUL SON, THAT CAN SO ASTONISH A MOTHER!
SHE DESIRES TO SPEAK WITH YOU IN HER CLOSET ERE YOU GO TO BED.
BUT IS THERE NO SEQUEL AT THE HEELS OF THIS MOTHER'S ADMIRATION? IMPART.
THUD
WE SHALL OBEY, WERE SHE TEN TIMES OUR MOTHER.
HAVE YOU ANY FURTHER TRADE WITH US?

MY LORD, YOU ONCE DID LOVE ME.
SO I DO STILL, BY THESE PICKERS AND STEALERS.
GOOD MY LORD, WHAT IS YOUR CAUSE OF DISTEMPER? YOU DO, SURELY, BAR THE DOOR UPON YOUR OWN LIBERTY, IF YOU DENY YOUR GRIEFS TO YOUR FRIEND.
SIR, I LACK ADVANCEMENT.

HOW CAN THAT BE, WHEN YOU HAVE THE VOICE OF THE KING HIMSELF FOR YOUR SUCCESSION IN DENMARK?
AY, BUT SIR, 'WHILE THE GRASS GROWS' - THE PROVERB IS SOMETHING MUSTY -

O, THE RECORDERS! LET ME SEE ONE.
!

TO WITHDRAW WITH YOU: WHY DO YOU GO ABOUT TO RECOVER THE WIND OF ME, AS IF YOU WOULD DRIVE ME INTO A TOIL?

O, MY LORD, IF MY DUTY BE TOO BOLD, MY LOVE IS TOO UNMANNERLY.
I DO NOT WELL UNDERSTAND THAT.
WILL YOU PLAY UPON THIS PIPE?

'TIS AS EASY AS LYING. GOVERN THESE VENTAGES WITH YOUR FINGERS AND THUMB, GIVE IT BREATH WITH YOUR MOUTH, AND IT WILL DISCOURSE MOST ELOQUENT MUSIC. LOOK YOU, THESE ARE THE STOPS.
BUT THESE CANNOT I COMMAND TO ANY UTTERANCE OF HARMONY; I HAVE NOT THE SKILL.
TUNK
WHY, LOOK YOU NOW, HOW UNWORTHY A THING YOU MAKE OF ME! YOU WOULD PLAY UPON ME; YOU WOULD SEEM TO KNOW MY STOPS; YOU WOULD PLUCK OUT THE HEART OF MY MYSTERY; YOU WOULD SOUND ME FROM MY LOWEST NOTE TO THE TOP OF MY COMPASS.
AND THERE IS MUCH MUSIC, EXCELLENT VOICE, IN THIS LITTLE ORGAN, YET CANNOT YOU MAKE IT SPEAK?
'SBLOOD, DO YOU THINK I AM EASIER TO BE PLAYED ON THAN A PIPE? CALL ME WHAT INSTRUMENT YOU WILL,
TUNK
TUNK
THOUGH YOU CAN FRET ME, YET YOU CANNOT PLAY UPON ME.

GOD BLESS YOU, SIR!
MY LORD, THE QUEEN WOULD SPEAK WITH YOU, AND PRESENTLY.
DO YOU SEE YONDER CLOUD THAT'S ALMOST IN SHAPE OF A CAMEL?
TMP TMP
TMP
BY THE MASS, AND 'TIS LIKE A CAMEL, INDEED.
METHINKS IT IS LIKE A WEASEL.

IT IS BACKED LIKE A WEASEL.
OR LIKE A WHALE?
VERY LIKE A WHALE.

SIGH
THEN I WILL COME TO MY MOTHER BY AND BY.
THEY FOOL ME TO THE TOP OF MY BENT.

...?
I WILL COME BY AND BY.

I WILL SAY SO.

BY AND BY IS EASILY SAID.

LEAVE ME, FRIENDS.
'TIS NOW THE VERY WITCHING TIME OF NIGHT, WHEN CHURCHYARDS YAWN AND HELL ITSELF BREATHES OUT CONTAGION TO THIS WORLD.
NOW COULD I DRINK HOT BLOOD, AND DO SUCH BITTER BUSINESS AS THE DAY WOULD QUAKE TO LOOK ON.

SOFT! NOW TO MY MOTHER.
O HEART, LOSE NOT THY NATURE; LET NOT EVER THE SOUL OF NERO ENTER THIS FIRM BOSOM. LET ME BE CRUEL, NOT UNNATURAL.
I WILL SPEAK DAGGERS TO HER, BUT USE NONE.
MY TONGUE AND SOUL IN THIS BE HYPOCRITES. HOW IN MY WORDS SOEVER SHE BE SHENT, TO GIVE THEM SEALS NEVER, MY SOUL, CONSENT!

ACT III
SCENE III
ANOTHER PART OF THE CASTLE.
I LIKE HIM NOT, NOR STANDS IT SAFE WITH US TO LET HIS MADNESS RANGE.

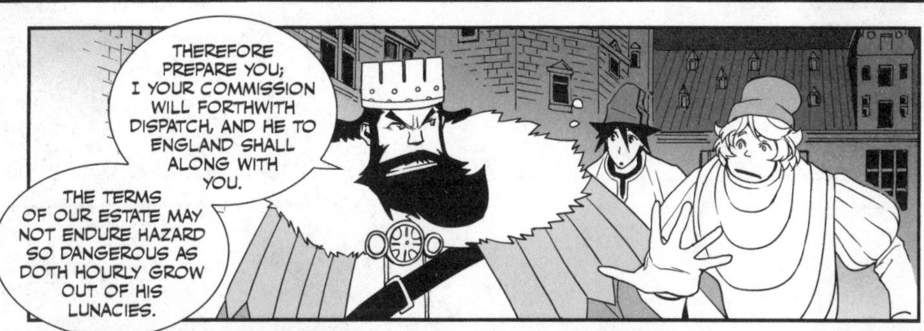
THEREFORE PREPARE YOU; I YOUR COMMISSION WILL FORTHWITH DISPATCH, AND HE TO ENGLAND SHALL ALONG WITH YOU.
THE TERMS OF OUR ESTATE MAY NOT ENDURE HAZARD SO DANGEROUS AS DOTH HOURLY GROW OUT OF HIS LUNACIES.

WE WILL OURSELVES PROVIDE. MOST HOLY AND RELIGIOUS FEAR IT IS TO KEEP THOSE MANY, MANY BODIES SAFE THAT LIVE AND FEED UPON YOUR MAJESTY.

THE SINGLE AND PECULIAR LIFE IS BOUND, WITH ALL THE STRENGTH AND ARMOUR OF THE MIND, TO KEEP ITSELF FROM NOYANCE; BUT MUCH MORE THAT SPIRIT UPON WHOSE WEAL DEPEND AND REST THE LIVES OF MANY.
THE CEASE OF MAJESTY DIES NOT ALONE, BUT, LIKE A GULF, DOTH DRAW WHAT'S NEAR IT WITH IT.

IT IS A MASSY WHEEL FIX'D ON THE SUMMIT OF THE HIGHEST MOUNT, TO WHOSE HUGE SPOKES TEN THOUSAND LESSER THINGS ARE MORTISED AND ADJOIN'D;
WHICH, WHEN IT FALLS, EACH SMALL ANNEXMENT, PETTY CONSEQUENCE, ATTENDS THE BOISTEROUS RUIN.
NEVER ALONE DID THE KING SIGH, BUT WITH A GENERAL GROAN.

WE WILL HASTE US.

ARM YOU, I PRAY YOU, TO THIS SPEEDY VOYAGE; FOR WE WILL FETTERS PUT UPON THIS FEAR, WHICH NOW GOES TOO FREE-FOOTED.

MY LORD, HE'S GOING TO HIS MOTHER'S CLOSET. BEHIND THE ARRAS I'LL CONVEY MYSELF, TO HEAR THE PROCESS.
I'LL WARRANT SHE'LL TAX HIM HOME.

I'LL CALL UPON YOU ERE YOU GO TO BED, AND TELL YOU WHAT I KNOW.
THANKS, DEAR MY LORD.

AND, AS YOU SAID (AND WISELY WAS IT SAID) 'TIS MEET THAT SOME MORE AUDIENCE THAN A MOTHER - SINCE NATURE MAKES THEM PARTIAL - SHOULD O'ERHEAR THE SPEECH, OF VANTAGE. FARE YOU WELL, MY LIEGE.

SCREEE-

O, MY OFFENCE IS RANK. IT SMELLS TO HEAVEN.

IT HATH THE PRIMAL ELDEST CURSE UPON 'T, A BROTHER'S MURDER.

PRAY CAN I NOT, THOUGH INCLINATION BE AS SHARP AS WILL,

MY STRONGER GUILT DEFEATS MY STRONG INTENT, AND, LIKE A MAN TO DOUBLE BUSINESS BOUND,

I STAND IN PAUSE WHERE I SHALL FIRST BEGIN, AND BOTH NEGLECT.

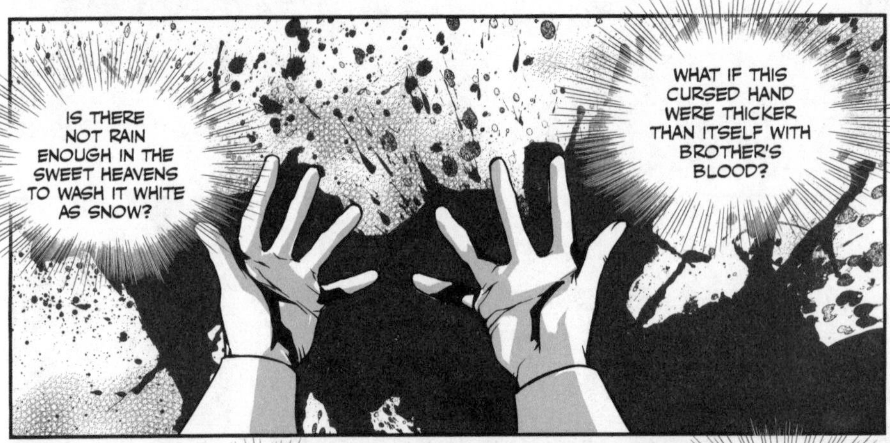

WHAT IF THIS CURSED HAND WERE THICKER THAN ITSELF WITH BROTHER'S BLOOD?
IS THERE NOT RAIN ENOUGH IN THE SWEET HEAVENS TO WASH IT WHITE AS SNOW?

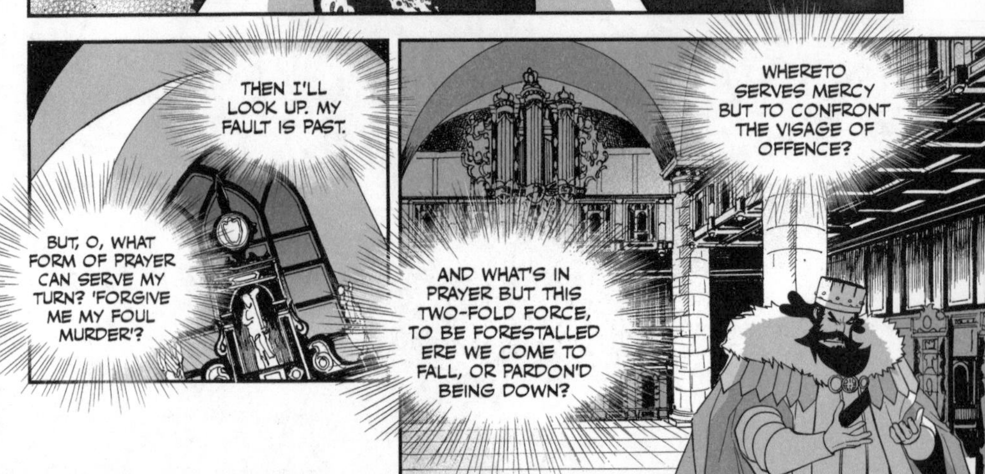

THEN I'LL LOOK UP. MY FAULT IS PAST.
BUT, O, WHAT FORM OF PRAYER CAN SERVE MY TURN? 'FORGIVE ME MY FOUL MURDER'?
WHERETO SERVES MERCY BUT TO CONFRONT THE VISAGE OF OFFENCE?
AND WHAT'S IN PRAYER BUT THIS TWO-FOLD FORCE, TO BE FORESTALLED ERE WE COME TO FALL, OR PARDON'D BEING DOWN?

THAT CANNOT BE, SINCE I AM STILL POSSESS'D OF THOSE EFFECTS FOR WHICH I DID THE MURDER: MY CROWN, MINE OWN AMBITION AND MY QUEEN.

MAY ONE BE PARDON'D AND RETAIN THE OFFENCE?

IN THE CORRUPTED CURRENTS OF THIS WORLD OFFENCE'S GILDED HAND MAY SHOVE BY JUSTICE, AND OFT 'TIS SEEN THE WICKED PRIZE ITSELF BUYS OUT THE LAW.

NRGH!

WHAT THEN? WHAT RESTS?

BUT 'TIS NOT SO ABOVE. THERE IS NO SHUFFLING. THERE THE ACTION LIES IN HIS TRUE NATURE, AND WE OURSELVES COMPELL'D, EVEN TO THE TEETH AND FOREHEAD OF OUR FAULTS, TO GIVE IN EVIDENCE.

TRY WHAT REPENTANCE CAN. WHAT CAN IT NOT?

YET WHAT CAN IT WHEN ONE CAN NOT REPENT?

O WRETCHED STATE!

O BOSOM BLACK AS DEATH! O LIMED SOUL, THAT, STRUGGLING TO BE FREE,

ART MORE ENGAGED!

HELP, ANGELS! MAKE ASSAY!

BOW, STUBBORN KNEES; AND, HEART WITH STRINGS OF STEEL, BE SOFT AS SINEWS OF THE NEWBORN BABE!

ALL MAY BE WELL.

TING!
NOW MIGHT I DO IT PAT. NOW HE IS PRAYING. AND NOW I'LL DO'T.
AND SO HE GOES TO HEAVEN. AND SO AM I REVENGED.
- THAT WOULD BE SCANN'D.
A VILLAIN KILLS MY FATHER, AND FOR THAT, I, HIS SOLE SON, DO THIS SAME VILLAIN SEND TO HEAVEN.
O, THIS IS HIRE AND SALARY, NOT REVENGE. HE TOOK MY FATHER GROSSLY, FULL OF BREAD,
WITH ALL HIS CRIMES BROAD BLOWN, AS FLUSH AS MAY. AND HOW HIS AUDIT STANDS WHO KNOWS SAVE HEAVEN?
BUT IN OUR CIRCUMSTANCE AND COURSE OF THOUGHT, 'TIS HEAVY WITH HIM.

AND AM I THEN REVENGED TO TAKE HIM IN THE PURGING OF HIS SOUL WHEN HE IS FIT AND SEASON'D FOR HIS PASSAGE?
NO!
UP, SWORD, AND KNOW THOU A MORE HORRID HENT.
SHHHH-
TIK.
WHEN HE IS DRUNK ASLEEP, OR IN HIS RAGE, OR IN THE INCESTUOUS PLEASURE OF HIS BED, AT GAMING, SWEARING, OR ABOUT SOME ACT THAT HAS NO RELISH OF SALVATION IN'T -

MY MOTHER STAYS:

THIS PHYSIC BUT PROLONGS THY SICKLY DAYS.

THEN TRIP HIM, THAT HIS HEELS MAY KICK AT HEAVEN, AND THAT HIS SOUL MAY BE AS DAMN'D AND BLACK AS HELL, WHERETO IT GOES.

MY WORDS FLY UP, MY THOUGHTS REMAIN BELOW. WORDS WITHOUT THOUGHTS NEVER TO HEAVEN GO.

ACT III
SCENE IV
THE QUEEN'S CLOSET

HE WILL COME STRAIGHT.

I'LL SILENCE ME EVEN HERE. PRAY YOU, BE ROUND WITH HIM.

LOOK YOU LAY HOME TO HIM: TELL HIM HIS PRANKS HAVE BEEN TOO BROAD TO BEAR WITH, AND THAT YOUR GRACE HATH SCREEN'D AND STOOD BETWEEN MUCH HEAT AND HIM.

MOTHER,
MOTHER,
MOTHER!
I'LL WARRANT YOU. FEAR ME NOT. WITHDRAW, I HEAR HIM COMING.

DASH!

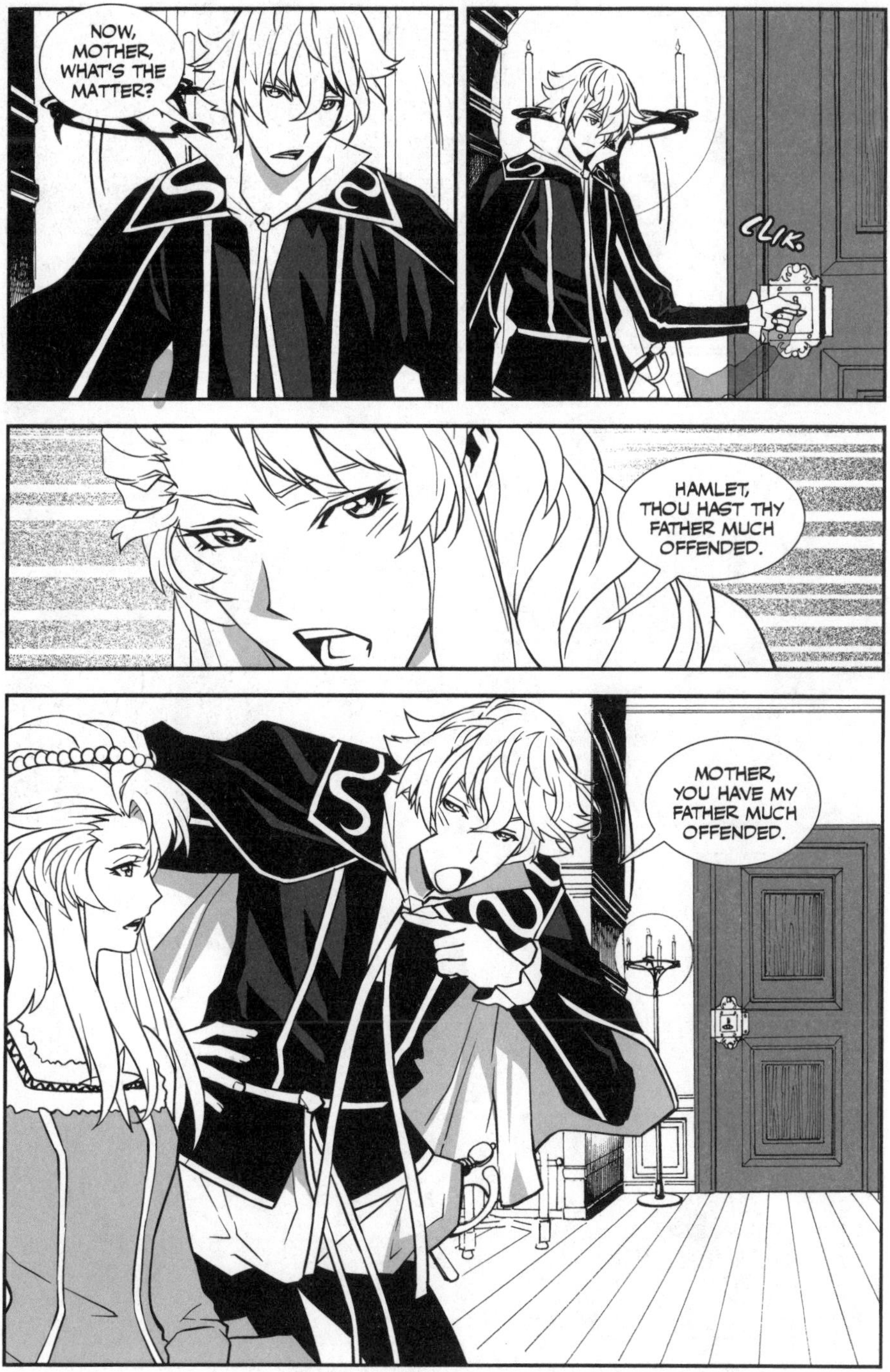

MOTHER, YOU HAVE MY FATHER MUCH OFFENDED.

GO, GO, YOU QUESTION WITH A WICKED TONGUE.
COME, COME, YOU ANSWER WITH AN IDLE TONGUE.
WHY, HOW NOW, HAMLET?
WHAT'S THE MATTER NOW?
HAVE YOU FORGOT ME?
NO, BY THE ROOD, NOT SO.

NAY, THEN, I'LL SET THOSE TO YOU THAT CAN SPEAK.
YOU ARE THE QUEEN, YOUR HUSBAND'S BROTHER'S WIFE, AND - WOULD IT WERE NOT SO! - YOU ARE MY MOTHER.
COME,
GRAB
COME,
AND SIT YOU DOWN.
FWUMP
YOU SHALL NOT BUDGE. YOU GO NOT TILL I SET YOU UP A GLASS WHERE YOU MAY SEE THE INMOST PART OF YOU.

WHAT WILT THOU DO?
THOU WILT NOT MURDER ME?
WHAT, HO?
!
HELP, HELP,
HELP!
SHING
HOW NOW! A RAT?
SHUNK!
SHUNK!

O ME,
WHAT HAST
THOU
DONE?

DEAD,
FOR A DUCAT,
DEAD!
O, I AM
SLAIN!

NAY,
I KNOW NOT.
IS IT THE
KING?
O, WHAT
A RASH AND
BLOODY DEED
IS THIS!

AY, LADY,
'TWAS MY
WORD.

AS KILL
A KING?

A BLOODY
DEED! ALMOST AS
BAD, GOOD MOTHER,
AS KILL A KING AND
MARRY WITH HIS
BROTHER.

THUD
!
NNN...
THOU WRETCHED, RASH, INTRUDING FOOL, FAREWELL! I TOOK THEE FOR THY BETTER. TAKE THY FORTUNE. THOU FIND'ST TO BE TOO BUSY IS SOME DANGER.

LEAVE WRINGING OF YOUR HANDS. PEACE!
SIT YOU DOWN AND LET ME WRING YOUR HEART. FOR SO I SHALL,
IF IT BE MADE OF PENETRABLE STUFF, IF DAMNED CUSTOM HAVE NOT BRASS'D IT SO THAT IT IS PROOF AND BULWARK AGAINST SENSE.
WHAT HAVE I DONE, THAT THOU DAREST WAG THY TONGUE IN NOISE SO RUDE AGAINST ME?

O, SUCH A DEED AS FROM THE BODY OF CONTRACTION PLUCKS THE VERY SOUL, AND SWEET RELIGION MAKES A RHAPSODY OF WORDS.
SUCH AN ACT THAT BLURS THE GRACE AND BLUSH OF MODESTY, CALLS VIRTUE HYPOCRITE, TAKES OFF THE ROSE FROM THE FAIR FOREHEAD OF AN INNOCENT LOVE AND SETS A BLISTER THERE,
MAKES MARRIAGE-VOWS AS FALSE AS DICERS' OATHS -
HEAVEN'S FACE DOTH GLOW O'ER THIS SOLIDITY AND COMPOUND MASS,WITH TRISTFUL VISAGE, AS AGAINST THE DOOM, IS THOUGHT-SICK AT THE ACT.

AY ME, WHAT ACT, THAT ROARS SO LOUD, AND THUNDERS IN THE INDEX?
LOOK HERE, UPON THIS PICTURE, AND ON THIS, THE COUNTERFEIT PRESENTMENT OF TWO BROTHERS.
SEE, WHAT A GRACE WAS SEATED ON THIS BROW;
HYPERION'S CURLS, THE FRONT OF JOVE HIMSELF, AN EYE LIKE MARS, TO THREATEN AND COMMAND;
A STATION LIKE THE HERALD MERCURY NEW-LIGHTED ON A HEAVEN-KISSING HILL;
A COMBINATION AND A FORM INDEED, WHERE EVERY GOD DID SEEM TO SET HIS SEAL, TO GIVE THE WORLD ASSURANCE OF A MAN.
THIS WAS YOUR HUSBAND.

LOOK YOU NOW, WHAT FOLLOWS: HERE IS YOUR HUSBAND,
LIKE A MILDEW'D EAR, BLASTING HIS WHOLESOME BROTHER.
AAAH!
HAVE YOU EYES?
COULD YOU ON THIS FAIR MOUNTAIN LEAVE TO FEED, AND BATTEN ON THIS MOOR?
HA! HAVE YOU EYES?
CLENCH

YOU CANNOT CALL IT LOVE; FOR AT YOUR AGE THE HEY-DAY IN THE BLOOD IS TAME, IT'S HUMBLE, AND WAITS UPON THE JUDGMENT:
AND WHAT JUDGMENT WOULD STEP FROM THIS TO THIS?

SENSE, SURE, YOU HAVE, ELSE COULD YOU NOT HAVE MOTION;

BUT SURE, THAT SENSE IS APOPLEX'D, FOR MADNESS WOULD NOT ERR,

NOR SENSE TO ECSTASY WAS NE'ER SO THRALL'D BUT IT RESERVED SOME QUANTITY OF CHOICE, TO SERVE IN SUCH A DIFFERENCE.

WHAT DEVIL WAS'T THAT THUS HATH COZEN'D YOU AT HOODMAN-BLIND?

EYES WITHOUT FEELING, FEELING WITHOUT SIGHT,
EARS WITHOUT HANDS OR EYES,
SMELLING SANS ALL, OR BUT A SICKLY PART OF ONE TRUE SENSE COULD NOT SO MOPE.
O SHAME! WHERE IS THY BLUSH?
REBELLIOUS HELL, IF THOU CANST MUTINE IN A MATRON'S BONES, TO FLAMING YOUTH LET VIRTUE BE AS WAX, AND MELT IN HER OWN FIRE.
PROCLAIM NO SHAME WHEN THE COMPULSIVE ARDOUR GIVES THE CHARGE, SINCE FROST ITSELF AS ACTIVELY DOTH BURN AND REASON PANDERS WILL.

O HAMLET, SPEAK NO MORE.

THOU TURN'ST MINE EYES INTO MY VERY SOUL, AND THERE I SEE SUCH BLACK AND GRAINED SPOTS AS WILL NOT LEAVE THEIR TINCT.

NAY, BUT TO LIVE IN THE RANK SWEAT OF AN ENSEAMED BED, STEW'D IN CORRUPTION, HONEYING AND MAKING LOVE OVER THE NASTY STY -

FWSSH

A MURDERER AND A VILLAIN; A SLAVE THAT IS NOT TWENTIETH PART THE TITHE OF YOUR PRECEDENT LORD.
A VICE OF KINGS, A CUTPURSE OF THE EMPIRE AND THE RULE, THAT FROM A SHELF THE PRECIOUS DIADEM STOLE, AND PUT IT IN HIS POCKET!
NO MORE!
A KING OF SHREDS AND PATCHES!
!!

WHAT WOULD YOUR GRACIOUS FIGURE?
ALAS, HE'S MAD!
SAVE ME, AND HOVER O'ER ME WITH YOUR WINGS, YOU HEAVENLY GUARDS!
DO YOU NOT COME YOUR TARDY SON TO CHIDE,
?!
THAT, LAPSED IN TIME AND PASSION, LETS GO BY THE IMPORTANT ACTING OF YOUR DREAD COMMAND?
O, SAY!

THIS VISITATION IS BUT TO WHET THY ALMOST BLUNTED PURPOSE.
DO NOT FORGET.
SPEAK TO HER, HAMLET.
HOW IS IT WITH YOU, LADY?
BUT LOOK, AMAZEMENT ON THY MOTHER SITS.
O, STEP BETWEEN HER AND HER FIGHTING SOUL. CONCEIT IN WEAKEST BODIES STRONGEST WORKS.
ALAS, HOW IS'T WITH YOU, THAT YOU DO BEND YOUR EYE ON VACANCY AND WITH THE INCORPORAL AIR DO HOLD DISCOURSE?

FORTH AT YOUR EYES YOUR SPIRITS WILDLY PEEP, AND, AS THE SLEEPING SOLDIERS IN THE ALARM, YOUR BEDDED HAIR, LIKE LIFE IN EXCREMENTS, STARTS UP, AND STANDS ON END.
O GENTLE SON, UPON THE HEAT AND FLAME OF THY DISTEMPER SPRINKLE COOL PATIENCE. WHEREON DO YOU LOOK?
?
ON HIM, ON HIM!
LOOK YOU, HOW PALE HE GLARES!
HIS FORM AND CAUSE CONJOIN'D, PREACHING TO STONES, WOULD MAKE THEM CAPABLE.

DO NOT LOOK UPON ME, LEST WITH THIS PITEOUS ACTION YOU CONVERT MY STERN EFFECTS.
THEN WHAT I HAVE TO DO WILL WANT TRUE COLOUR; TEARS PERCHANCE FOR BLOOD.
TO WHOM DO YOU SPEAK THIS?
NOTHING AT ALL; YET ALL THAT IS I SEE.
DO YOU SEE NOTHING THERE?
NOR DID YOU NOTHING HEAR?

NO, NOTHING BUT OURSELVES.
SSSSSH-
WHY, LOOK YOU THERE! LOOK HOW IT STEALS AWAY!

?
MY FATHER, IN HIS HABIT AS HE LIVED!
LOOK, WHERE HE GOES, EVEN NOW, OUT AT THE PORTAL!

THIS IS THE VERY COINAGE OF YOUR BRAIN. THIS BODILESS CREATION ECSTASY IS VERY CUNNING IN.

MY PULSE, AS YOURS, DOTH TEMPERATELY KEEP TIME, AND MAKES AS HEALTHFUL MUSIC.

IT IS NOT MADNESS THAT I HAVE UTTER'D.

ECSTASY!

IT WILL BUT SKIN AND FILM THE ULCEROUS PLACE, WHILST RANK CORRUPTION, MINING ALL WITHIN, INFECTS UNSEEN.
CONFESS YOURSELF TO HEAVEN, REPENT WHAT'S PAST, AVOID WHAT IS TO COME;
AND DO NOT SPREAD THE COMPOST ON THE WEEDS, TO MAKE THEM RANKER.
FORGIVE ME THIS MY VIRTUE; FOR IN THE FATNESS OF THESE PURSY TIMES VIRTUE ITSELF OF VICE MUST PARDON BEG, YEA, CURB AND WOO FOR LEAVE TO DO HIM GOOD.
O HAMLET, THOU HAST CLEFT MY HEART IN TWAIN.
O, THROW AWAY THE WORSER PART OF IT, AND LIVE THE PURER WITH THE OTHER HALF.

THAT MONSTER, CUSTOM, WHO ALL SENSE DOTH EAT, OF HABITS EVIL, IS ANGEL YET IN THIS,
THAT TO THE USE OF ACTIONS FAIR AND GOOD HE LIKEWISE GIVES A FROCK OR LIVERY THAT APTLY IS PUT ON.

GOOD NIGHT. BUT GO NOT TO MINE UNCLE'S BED.
ASSUME A VIRTUE, IF YOU HAVE IT NOT.

REFRAIN TONIGHT, AND THAT SHALL LEND A KIND OF EASINESS TO THE NEXT ABSTINENCE. THE NEXT MORE EASY;

FOR USE ALMOST CAN CHANGE THE STAMP OF NATURE, AND EITHER SHAME THE DEVIL, OR THROW HIM OUT WITH WONDROUS POTENCY.

ONCE MORE, GOOD NIGHT,

AND WHEN YOU ARE DESIROUS TO BE BLESS'D, I'LL BLESSING BEG OF YOU.

FOR THIS SAME LORD, I DO REPENT;
BUT HEAVEN HATH PLEASED IT SO, TO PUNISH ME WITH THIS, AND THIS WITH ME, THAT I MUST BE THEIR SCOURGE AND MINISTER.
I WILL BESTOW HIM, AND WILL ANSWER WELL THE DEATH I GAVE HIM.
SO, AGAIN, GOOD NIGHT.
WHAT SHALL I DO?
I MUST BE CRUEL, ONLY TO BE KIND: THUS BAD BEGINS AND WORSE REMAINS BEHIND.
ONE WORD MORE, GOOD LADY.
NOT THIS, BY NO MEANS, THAT I BID YOU DO:
SQUEEEZE

LET THE BLOAT KING TEMPT YOU AGAIN TO BED, PINCH WANTON ON YOUR CHEEK, CALL YOU HIS MOUSE,
AND LET HIM, FOR A PAIR OF REECHY KISSES, OR PADDLING IN YOUR NECK WITH HIS DAMN'D FINGERS,
MAKE YOU TO RAVEL ALL THIS MATTER OUT, THAT I ESSENTIALLY AM NOT IN MADNESS, BUT MAD IN CRAFT.
'TWERE GOOD YOU LET HIM KNOW, FOR WHO THAT'S BUT A QUEEN, FAIR, SOBER, WISE, WOULD FROM A PADDOCK, FROM A BAT, A GIB, SUCH DEAR CONCERNINGS HIDE? WHO WOULD DO SO?

NO, IN DESPITE OF SENSE AND SECRECY, UNPEG THE BASKET ON THE HOUSE'S TOP. LET THE BIRDS FLY, AND, LIKE THE FAMOUS APE, TO TRY CONCLUSIONS, IN THE BASKET CREEP, AND BREAK YOUR OWN NECK DOWN.
BE THOU ASSURED,
IF WORDS BE MADE OF BREATH, AND BREATH OF LIFE, I HAVE NO LIFE TO BREATHE WHAT THOU HAST SAID TO ME.
DRIP
I MUST TO ENGLAND, YOU KNOW THAT?
ALACK, I HAD FORGOT. 'TIS SO CONCLUDED ON.
SHFF

CLIK
LET IT WORK; FOR 'TIS THE SPORT TO HAVE THE ENGINEER HOIST WITH HIS OWN PETARD,
THERE'S LETTERS SEAL'D:
AND 'T SHALL GO HARD BUT I WILL DELVE ONE YARD BELOW THEIR MINES, AND BLOW THEM AT THE MOON.
AND MY TWO SCHOOL-FELLOWS, WHOM I WILL TRUST AS I WILL ADDERS FANG'D,
THEY BEAR THE MANDATE, THEY MUST SWEEP MY WAY, AND MARSHAL ME TO KNAVERY.
O, 'TIS MOST SWEET, WHEN IN ONE LINE TWO CRAFTS DIRECTLY MEET.
THIS MAN SHALL SET ME PACKING.
SSSSH

I'LL LUG THE GUTS INTO THE NEIGHBOUR ROOM.
MOTHER, GOOD NIGHT. INDEED THIS COUNSELLOR IS NOW MOST STILL, MOST SECRET AND MOST GRAVE, WHO WAS IN LIFE A FOOLISH PRATING KNAVE.
SSHHHHHH

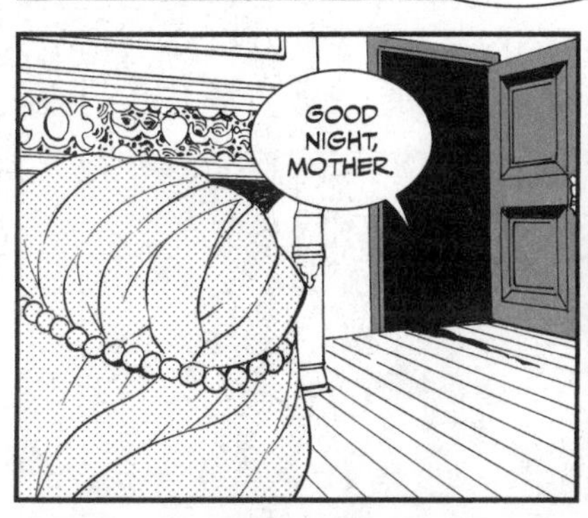
GOOD NIGHT, MOTHER.

COME, SIR, TO DRAW TOWARD AN END WITH YOU.
SSHH-

ACT IV
SCENE I

THERE'S MATTER IN THESE SIGHS. THESE PROFOUND HEAVES YOU MUST TRANSLATE.

'TIS FIT WE UNDERSTAND THEM.
WHERE IS YOUR SON?
BESTOW THIS PLACE ON US A LITTLE WHILE.

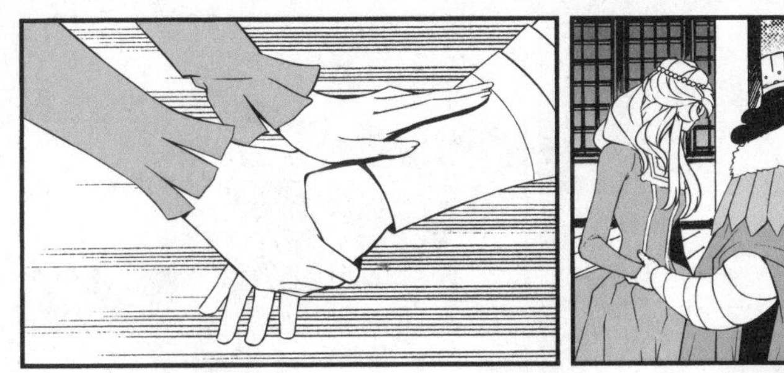

AH, MY GOOD LORD, WHAT HAVE I SEEN TONIGHT!
WHAT, GERTRUDE? HOW DOES HAMLET?
MAD AS THE SEA AND WIND, WHEN BOTH CONTEND WHICH IS THE MIGHTIER.

SOB

IN HIS LAWLESS FIT, BEHIND THE ARRAS HEARING SOMETHING STIR, WHIPS OUT HIS RAPIER, CRIES 'A RAT, A RAT!'

AND, IN THIS BRAINISH APPREHENSION, KILLS THE UNSEEN GOOD OLD MAN.

IT HAD BEEN SO WITH US, HAD WE BEEN THERE.

O HEAVY DEED!

ALAS, HOW SHALL THIS BLOODY DEED BE ANSWER'D?

HIS LIBERTY IS FULL OF THREATS TO ALL; TO YOU YOURSELF, TO US, TO EVERYONE.

IT WILL BE LAID TO US, WHOSE PROVIDENCE SHOULD HAVE KEPT SHORT, RESTRAIN'D AND OUT OF HAUNT THIS MAD YOUNG MAN.
BUT SO MUCH WAS OUR LOVE WE WOULD NOT UNDERSTAND WHAT WAS MOST FIT; BUT, LIKE THE OWNER OF A FOUL DISEASE, TO KEEP IT FROM DIVULGING, LET IT FEED EVEN ON THE PITH OF LIFE.

WHERE IS HE GONE?

TO DRAW APART THE BODY HE HATH KILL'D, O'ER WHOM HIS VERY MADNESS, LIKE SOME ORE AMONG A MINERAL OF METALS BASE, SHOWS ITSELF PURE.

HE WEEPS FOR WHAT IS DONE.

O GERTRUDE, COME AWAY!

THE SUN NO SOONER SHALL THE MOUNTAINS TOUCH, BUT WE WILL SHIP HIM HENCE,

AND THIS VILE DEED WE MUST, WITH ALL OUR MAJESTY AND SKILL, BOTH COUNTENANCE AND EXCUSE.

HO, GUILDENSTERN!

FRIENDS BOTH, GO JOIN YOU WITH SOME FURTHER AID:

HAMLET IN MADNESS HATH POLONIUS SLAIN, AND FROM HIS MOTHER'S CLOSET HATH HE DRAGG'D HIM.

GO SEEK HIM OUT, SPEAK FAIR, AND BRING THE BODY INTO THE CHAPEL.
I PRAY YOU, HASTE IN THIS.

COME, GERTRUDE, WE'LL CALL UP OUR WISEST FRIENDS, AND LET THEM KNOW BOTH WHAT WE MEAN TO DO, AND WHAT'S UNTIMELY DONE.

SO DREADED SLANDER - WHOSE WHISPER O'ER THE WORLD'S DIAMETER, AS LEVEL AS THE CANNON TO HIS BLANK, TRANSPORTS THE POISONED SHOT, MAY MISS OUR NAME, AND HIT THE WOUNDLESS AIR.
O, COME AWAY!
MY SOUL IS FULL OF DISCORD AND DISMAY.
HAAAAH...
ACT IV
SCENE II
ANOTHER PART OF THE CASTLE.
SAFELY STOWED.

HM?
O, HERE THEY COME.

HAMLET! LORD HAMLET!
WHAT NOISE? WHO CALLS ON HAMLET?

WHAT HAVE YOU DONE, MY LORD, WITH THE DEAD BODY?

COMPOUNDED IT WITH DUST, WHERETO 'TIS KIN.

DO NOT BELIEVE IT.

BELIEVE WHAT?
TELL US WHERE 'TIS, THAT WE MAY TAKE IT THENCE AND BEAR IT TO THE CHAPEL.

WHAT REPLICATION SHOULD BE MADE BY THE SON OF A KING?
THAT I CAN KEEP YOUR COUNSEL AND NOT MINE OWN.
BESIDES, TO BE DEMANDED OF A SPONGE!
TAKE YOU ME FOR A SPONGE, MY LORD?
AY, SIR, THAT SOAKS UP THE KING'S COUNTENANCE, HIS REWARDS, HIS AUTHORITIES.
BUT SUCH OFFICERS DO THE KING BEST SERVICE IN THE END:
HE KEEPS THEM, LIKE AN APE, IN THE CORNER OF HIS JAW; FIRST MOUTHED, TO BE LAST SWALLOWED:
WHEN HE NEEDS WHAT YOU HAVE GLEANED, IT IS BUT SQUEEZING YOU, AND, SPONGE, YOU SHALL BE DRY AGAIN.

I AM GLAD OF IT.
A KNAVISH SPEECH SLEEPS IN A FOOLISH EAR.
THUMP

I UNDERSTAND YOU NOT, MY LORD.

MY LORD, YOU MUST TELL US WHERE THE BODY IS, AND GO WITH US TO THE KING.

THE BODY IS WITH THE KING, BUT THE KING IS NOT WITH THE BODY.

THE KING IS A THING -

HUP!

A THING, MY LORD!

HIDE FOX,
THUMP

SHUF
OF NOTHING. BRING ME TO HIM.

AND ALL AFTER.
DASH!

I HAVE SENT TO SEEK HIM, AND TO FIND THE BODY.
ACT IV
SCENE III

YET MUST NOT WE PUT THE STRONG LAW ON HIM: HE'S LOVED OF THE DISTRACTED MULTITUDE, WHO LIKE NOT IN THEIR JUDGMENT, BUT THEIR EYES;
HOW DANGEROUS IS IT THAT THIS MAN GOES LOOSE!

AND WHERE 'TIS SO, THE OFFENDER'S SCOURGE IS WEIGH'D, BUT NEVER THE OFFENCE.
TO BEAR ALL SMOOTH AND EVEN, THIS SUDDEN SENDING HIM AWAY MUST SEEM DELIBERATE PAUSE. DISEASES DESPERATE GROWN BY DESPERATE APPLIANCE ARE RELIEVED, OR NOT AT ALL.

WHERE THE DEAD BODY IS BESTOW'D, MY LORD, WE CANNOT GET FROM HIM.
HOW NOW! WHAT HATH BEFALL'N?
BAM!

WITHOUT, MY LORD, GUARDED, TO KNOW YOUR PLEASURE.

BRING HIM BEFORE US.

HO, GUILDENSTERN!

BUT WHERE IS HE?

GRAB

BRING IN MY LORD.

SMACK!

NOW, HAMLET, WHERE'S POLONIUS?
AT SUPPER.
AT SUPPER! WHERE?
NOT WHERE HE EATS, BUT WHERE HE IS EATEN.
A CERTAIN CONVOCATION OF POLITIC WORMS ARE E'EN AT HIM. YOUR WORM IS YOUR ONLY EMPEROR FOR DIET.
WE FAT ALL CREATURES ELSE TO FAT US, AND WE FAT OURSELVES FOR MAGGOTS.
ALAS, ALAS!
YOUR FAT KING AND YOUR LEAN BEGGAR IS BUT VARIABLE SERVICE - TWO DISHES, BUT TO ONE TABLE. THAT'S THE END.

A MAN MAY FISH WITH THE WORM THAT HATH EAT OF A KING,
AND EAT OF THE FISH THAT HATH FED OF THAT WORM.
WHAT DOST THOU MEAN BY THIS?
NOTHING BUT TO SHOW YOU HOW A KING MAY GO A PROGRESS THROUGH THE GUTS OF A BEGGAR.
WHERE IS POLONIUS?

IN HEAVEN. SEND HITHER TO SEE. IF YOUR MESSENGER FIND HIM NOT THERE, SEEK HIM I' THE OTHER PLACE YOURSELF.
BUT INDEED, IF YOU FIND HIM NOT WITHIN THIS MONTH, YOU SHALL NOSE HIM AS YOU GO UP THE STAIRS INTO THE LOBBY.
HAMLET, THIS DEED, FOR THINE ESPECIAL SAFETY - WHICH WE DO TENDER, AS WE DEARLY GRIEVE FOR THAT WHICH THOU HAST DONE - MUST SEND THEE HENCE WITH FIERY QUICKNESS.
THEREFORE PREPARE THYSELF;
GO SEEK HIM THERE!
HE WILL STAY TILL YE COME.

THE BARK IS READY, AND THE WIND AT HELP, THE ASSOCIATES TEND, AND EVERY THING IS BENT FOR ENGLAND.
FOR ENGLAND!
GOOD.
SO IS IT, IF THOU KNEW'ST OUR PURPOSES.
AY, HAMLET.
I SEE A CHERUB THAT SEES THEM.
BUT, COME; FOR ENGLAND!
FAREWELL, DEAR MOTHER.

MY MOTHER.
THY LOVING FATHER, HAMLET.
COME, FOR ENGLAND!
HUP
HUP
FATHER AND MOTHER IS MAN AND WIFE; MAN AND WIFE IS ONE FLESH; AND SO, MY MOTHER.
FOLLOW HIM AT FOOT. TEMPT HIM WITH SPEED ABOARD; DELAY IT NOT; I'LL HAVE HIM HENCE TO-NIGHT.

AND, ENGLAND, IF MY LOVE THOU HOLD'ST AT AUGHT - AS MY GREAT POWER THEREOF MAY GIVE THEE SENSE, SINCE YET THY CICATRICE LOOKS RAW AND RED AFTER THE DANISH SWORD, AND THY FREE AWE PAYS HOMAGE TO US -

THOU MAYST NOT COLDLY SET OUR SOVEREIGN PROCESS, WHICH IMPORTS AT FULL, BY LETTERS CONJURING TO THAT EFFECT, THE PRESENT DEATH OF HAMLET.

DO IT, ENGLAND; FOR LIKE THE HECTIC IN MY BLOOD HE RAGES, AND THOU MUST CURE ME.

TILL I KNOW 'TIS DONE, HOWE'ER MY HAPS, MY JOYS WERE NE'ER BEGUN.

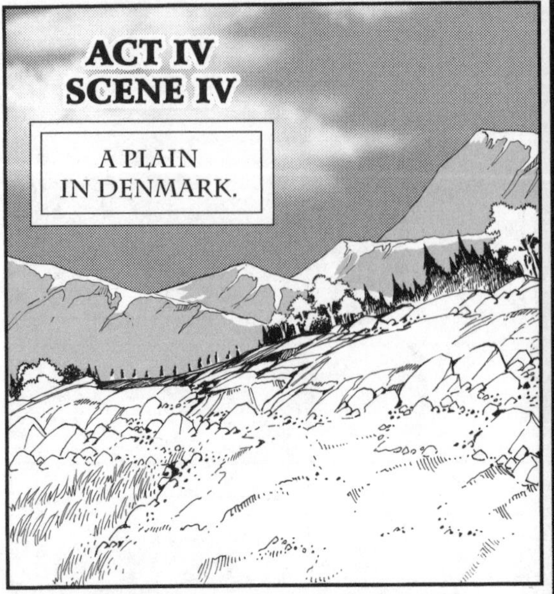

ACT IV
SCENE IV
A PLAIN IN DENMARK.

GO, CAPTAIN, FROM ME GREET THE DANISH KING.
TELL HIM THAT, BY HIS LICENSE, FORTINBRAS CRAVES THE CONVEYANCE OF A PROMISED MARCH OVER HIS KINGDOM.
YOU KNOW THE RENDEZVOUS.
IF THAT HIS MAJESTY WOULD AUGHT WITH US, WE SHALL EXPRESS OUR DUTY IN HIS EYE; AND LET HIM KNOW SO.
FORTINBRAS

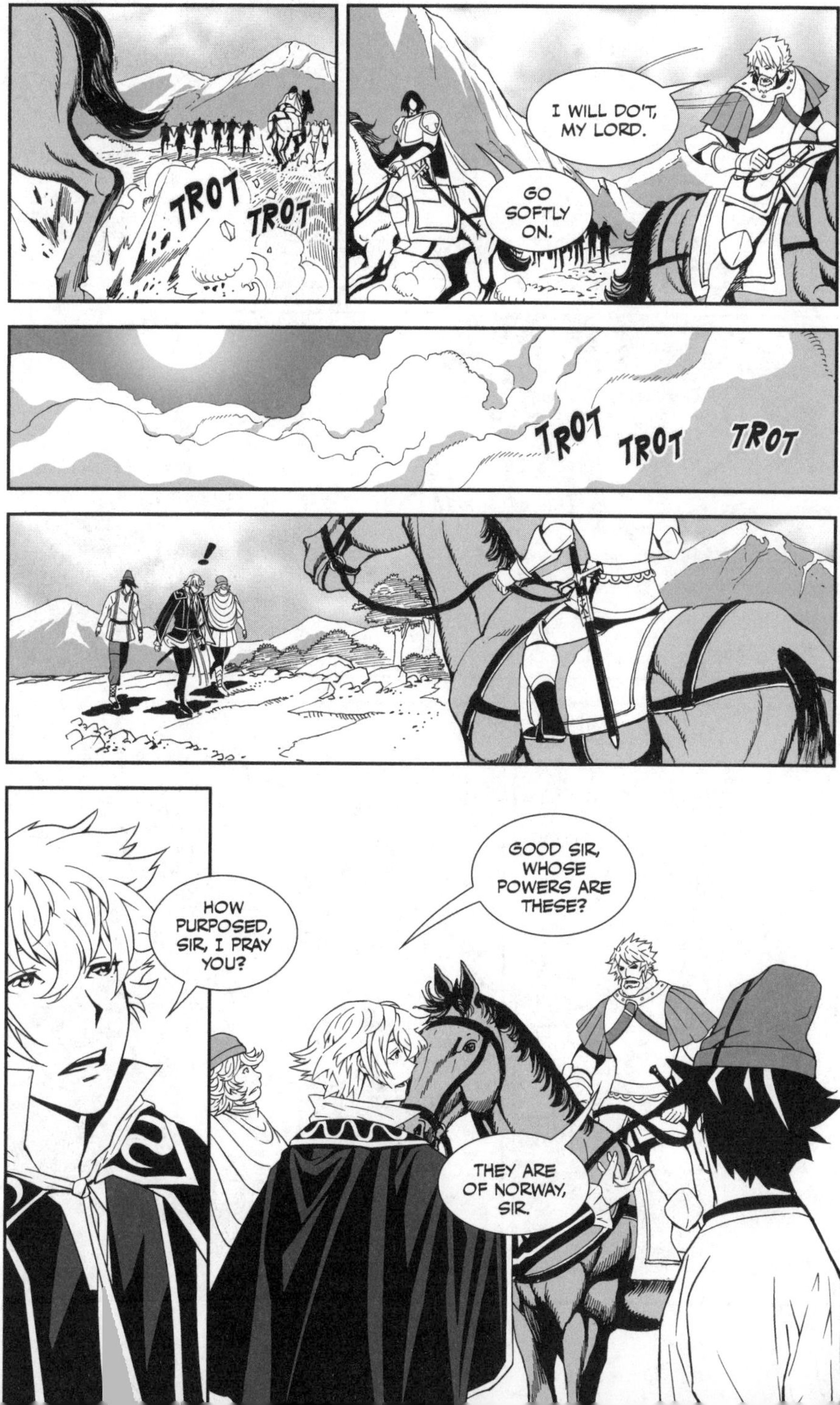

I WILL DO'T, MY LORD.
GO SOFTLY ON.

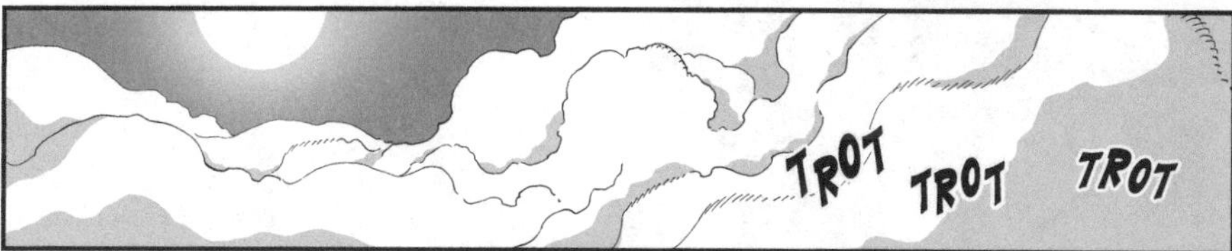

GOOD SIR, WHOSE POWERS ARE THESE?

THEY ARE OF NORWAY, SIR.

HOW PURPOSED, SIR, I PRAY YOU?

WHO COMMANDS THEM, SIR?

AGAINST SOME PART OF POLAND.

THE NEPHEW TO OLD NORWAY, FORTINBRAS.

TO PAY FIVE DUCATS, FIVE, I WOULD NOT FARM IT; NOR WILL IT YIELD TO NORWAY OR THE POLE A RANKER RATE, SHOULD IT BE SOLD IN FEE.

GOES IT AGAINST THE MAIN OF POLAND, SIR, OR FOR SOME FRONTIER?
TRULY TO SPEAK, AND WITH NO ADDITION, WE GO TO GAIN A LITTLE PATCH OF GROUND THAT HATH IN IT NO PROFIT BUT THE NAME.

YES, IT IS ALREADY GARRISON'D.
WHY, THEN THE POLACK NEVER WILL DEFEND IT.
TWO THOUSAND SOULS AND TWENTY THOUSAND DUCATS WILL NOT DEBATE THE QUESTION OF THIS STRAW!
THIS IS THE IMPOSTHUME OF MUCH WEALTH AND PEACE, THAT INWARD BREAKS, AND SHOWS NO CAUSE WITHOUT WHY THE MAN DIES.
I HUMBLY THANK YOU, SIR.
GOD BE WI' YOU, SIR.

GO A LITTLE BEFORE.

WILL'T PLEASE YOU GO, MY LORD?
I'LL BE WITH YOU STRAIGHT.

HOW ALL OCCASIONS DO INFORM AGAINST ME, AND SPUR MY DULL REVENGE!

RRRGH
WHAT IS A MAN, IF HIS CHIEF GOOD AND MARKET OF HIS TIME BE BUT TO SLEEP AND FEED? A BEAST, NO MORE.
SURE HE THAT MADE US WITH SUCH LARGE DISCOURSE, LOOKING BEFORE AND AFTER, GAVE US NOT THAT CAPABILITY AND GOD-LIKE REASON TO FUST IN US UNUSED.

EXAMPLES GROSS AS EARTH EXHORT ME:
WITNESS THIS ARMY OF SUCH MASS AND CHARGE,
LED BY A DELICATE AND TENDER PRINCE, WHOSE SPIRIT, WITH DIVINE AMBITION PUFF'D, MAKES MOUTHS AT THE INVISIBLE EVENT,
EXPOSING WHAT IS MORTAL AND UNSURE TO ALL THAT FORTUNE, DEATH AND DANGER DARE, EVEN FOR AN EGG-SHELL.
RIGHTLY TO BE GREAT IS NOT TO STIR WITHOUT GREAT ARGUMENT, BUT GREATLY TO FIND QUARREL IN A STRAW WHEN HONOUR'S AT THE STAKE.
NOW, WHETHER IT BE BESTIAL OBLIVION, OR SOME CRAVEN SCRUPLE OF THINKING TOO PRECISELY ON THE EVENT -
A THOUGHT WHICH, QUARTER'D, HATH BUT ONE PART WISDOM AND EVER THREE PARTS COWARD -
I DO NOT KNOW WHY YET I LIVE TO SAY 'THIS THING'S TO DO', SITH I HAVE CAUSE, AND WILL, AND STRENGTH, AND MEANS TO DO'T.

HOW STAND I THEN, THAT HAVE A FATHER KILL'D, A MOTHER STAIN'D, EXCITEMENTS OF MY REASON AND MY BLOOD, AND LET ALL SLEEP,
WHILE, TO MY SHAME, I SEE THE IMMINENT DEATH OF TWENTY THOUSAND MEN, THAT, FOR A FANTASY AND TRICK OF FAME, GO TO THEIR GRAVES LIKE BEDS, FIGHT FOR A PLOT WHEREON THE NUMBERS CANNOT TRY THE CAUSE, WHICH IS NOT TOMB ENOUGH AND CONTINENT TO HIDE THE SLAIN?
O, FROM THIS TIME FORTH, MY THOUGHTS BE BLOODY OR BE NOTHING WORTH!

ACT IV SCENE V

ELSINORE. A ROOM IN THE CASTLE.

I WILL NOT SPEAK WITH HER.

SHE IS IMPORTUNATE, INDEED DISTRACT. HER MOOD WILL NEEDS BE PITIED.

WHAT WOULD SHE HAVE?

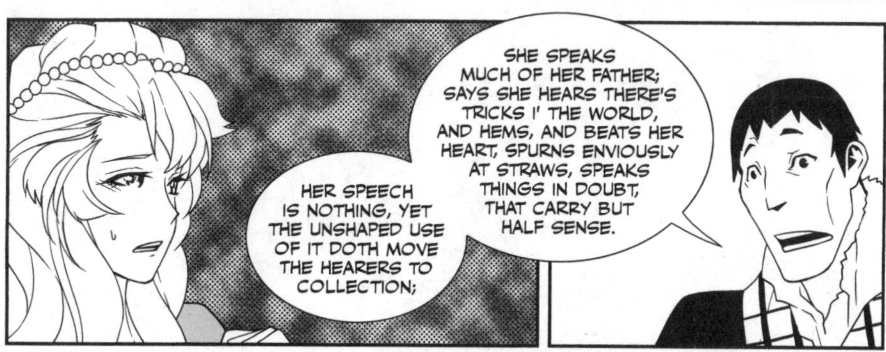

SHE SPEAKS MUCH OF HER FATHER; SAYS SHE HEARS THERE'S TRICKS I' THE WORLD, AND HEMS, AND BEATS HER HEART, SPURNS ENVIOUSLY AT STRAWS, SPEAKS THINGS IN DOUBT, THAT CARRY BUT HALF SENSE.
HER SPEECH IS NOTHING, YET THE UNSHAPED USE OF IT DOTH MOVE THE HEARERS TO COLLECTION;

THEY AIM AT IT, AND BOTCH THE WORDS UP FIT TO THEIR OWN THOUGHTS, WHICH, AS HER WINKS, AND NODS, AND GESTURES YIELD THEM, INDEED WOULD MAKE ONE THINK THERE MIGHT BE THOUGHT, THOUGH NOTHING SURE, YET MUCH UNHAPPILY.
'TWERE GOOD SHE WERE SPOKEN WITH, FOR SHE MAY STREW DANGEROUS CONJECTURES IN ILL-BREEDING MINDS.

LET HER COME IN.
TO MY SICK SOUL, AS SIN'S TRUE NATURE IS, EACH TOY SEEMS PROLOGUE TO SOME GREAT AMISS.
SO FULL OF ARTLESS JEALOUSY IS GUILT, IT SPILLS ITSELF IN FEARING TO BE SPILT.

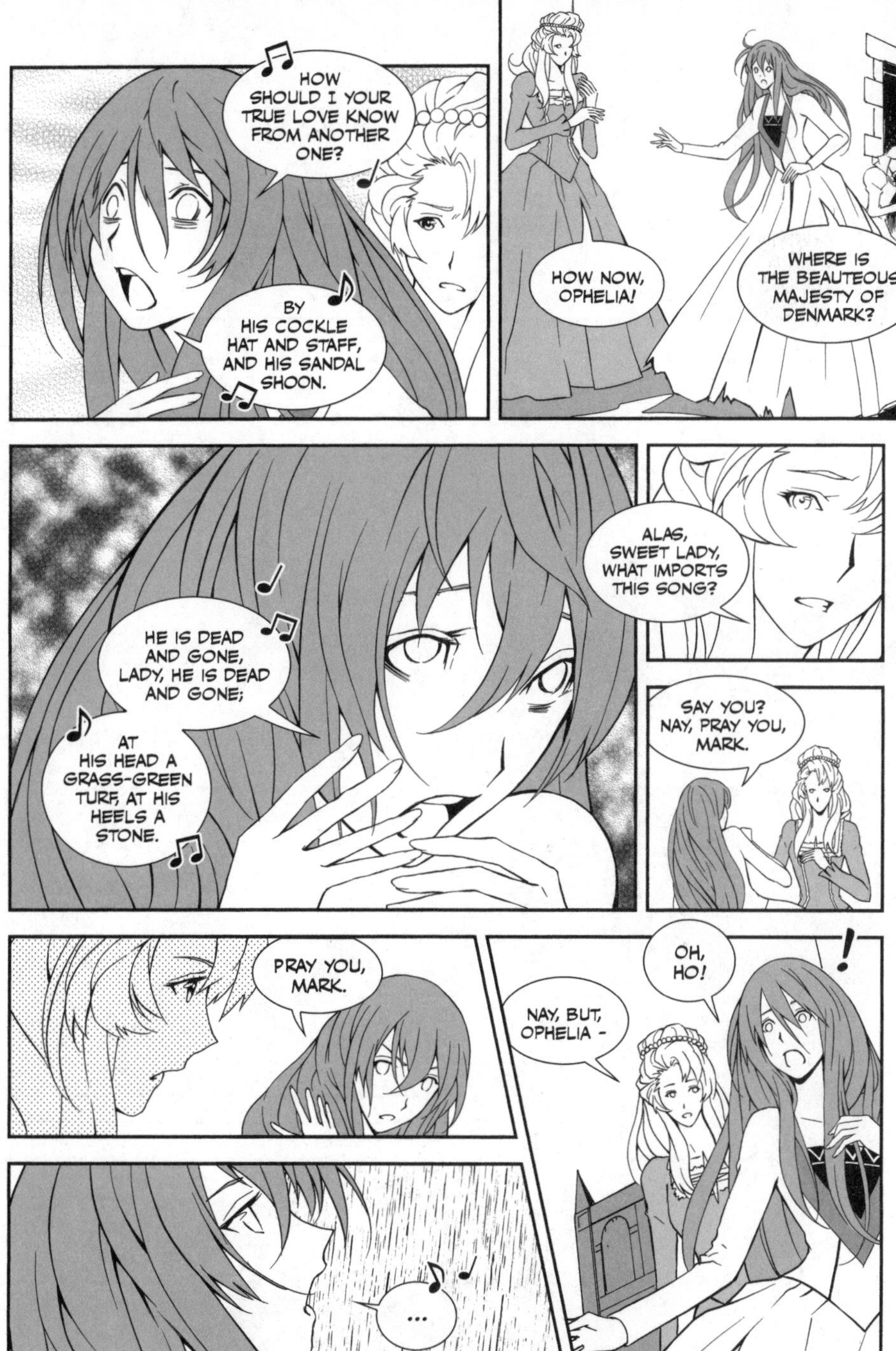
HOW SHOULD I YOUR TRUE LOVE KNOW FROM ANOTHER ONE?
BY HIS COCKLE HAT AND STAFF, AND HIS SANDAL SHOON.
HOW NOW, OPHELIA!
WHERE IS THE BEAUTEOUS MAJESTY OF DENMARK?
HE IS DEAD AND GONE, LADY, HE IS DEAD AND GONE;
AT HIS HEAD A GRASS-GREEN TURF, AT HIS HEELS A STONE.
ALAS, SWEET LADY, WHAT IMPORTS THIS SONG?
SAY YOU? NAY, PRAY YOU, MARK.
PRAY YOU, MARK.
...
OH, HO!
!
NAY, BUT, OPHELIA -

AH!
WHITE HIS SHROUD AS THE MOUNTAIN SNOW -
ALAS, LOOK HERE, MY LORD.
LARDED ALL WITH SWEET FLOWERS, WHICH BEWEPT TO THE GROUND DID NOT GO WITH TRUE-LOVE SHOWERS.
HOW DO YOU, PRETTY LADY?

LORD, WE KNOW WHAT WE ARE, BUT KNOW NOT WHAT WE MAY BE. GOD BE AT YOUR TABLE!
WELL, GOD 'ILD YOU!
THEY SAY THE OWL WAS A BAKER'S DAUGHTER.

PRAY YOU,

CONCEIT UPON HER FATHER.

LET'S HAVE NO WORDS OF THIS,
BUT WHEN THEY ASK YOU WHAT IT MEANS, SAY YOU THIS:

INDEED, LA, WITHOUT AN OATH, I'LL MAKE AN END ON'T:
PRETTY OPHELIA!
BY GIS AND BY SAINT CHARITY, ALACK, AND FIE FOR SHAME! YOUNG MEN WILL DO'T, IF THEY COME TO'T; BY COCK, THEY ARE TO BLAME.
QUOTH SHE, BEFORE YOU TUMBLED ME, YOU PROMISED ME TO WED.
TO-MORROW IS SAINT VALENTINE'S DAY, ALL IN THE MORNING BETIME, AND I A MAID AT YOUR WINDOW, TO BE YOUR VALENTINE.
THEN UP HE ROSE, AND DONN'D HIS CLOTHES, AND DUPP'D THE CHAMBER-DOOR; LET IN THE MAID, THAT OUT A MAID NEVER DEPARTED MORE.

HE ANSWERS,
SO WOULD I HA' DONE, BY YONDER SUN, AN THOU HADST NOT COME TO MY BED.
I HOPE ALL WILL BE WELL. WE MUST BE PATIENT; BUT I CANNOT CHOOSE BUT WEEP, TO THINK THEY SHOULD LAY HIM I' THE COLD GROUND.
NNH...
HOW LONG HATH SHE BEEN THUS?
MY BROTHER SHALL KNOW OF IT: AND SO I THANK YOU FOR YOUR GOOD COUNSEL.

GOOD NIGHT, LADIES; GOOD NIGHT, SWEET LADIES; GOOD NIGHT, GOOD NIGHT.
COME, MY COACH!
PAT PAT
PAT
O GERTRUDE, GERTRUDE, WHEN SORROWS COME, THEY COME NOT SINGLE SPIES BUT IN BATTALIONS.
FOLLOW HER CLOSE; GIVE HER GOOD WATCH, I PRAY YOU.
O, THIS IS THE POISON OF DEEP GRIEF; IT SPRINGS ALL FROM HER FATHER'S DEATH.
FIRST, HER FATHER SLAIN; NEXT, YOUR SON GONE; AND HE MOST VIOLENT AUTHOR OF HIS OWN JUST REMOVE;

AND WANTS NOT BUZZERS TO INFECT HIS EAR WITH PESTILENT SPEECHES OF HIS FATHER'S DEATH; WHEREIN NECESSITY, OF MATTER BEGGAR'D, WILL NOTHING STICK OUR PERSON TO ARRAIGN IN EAR AND EAR.
O MY DEAR GERTRUDE, THIS, LIKE TO A MURDERING-PIECE, IN MANY PLACES GIVES ME SUPERFLUOUS DEATH.
BAM!
BAM!
ALACK, WHAT NOISE IS THIS?
WHERE ARE MY SWITZERS? LET THEM GUARD THE DOOR.
WHAT IS THE MATTER?
SAVE YOURSELF, MY LORD.
THE PEOPLE MUDDIED, THICK AND UNWHOLESOME IN THEIR THOUGHTS AND WHISPERS, FOR GOOD POLONIUS' DEATH; AND WE HAVE DONE BUT GREENLY IN HUGGER-MUGGER TO INTER HIM.
POOR OPHELIA DIVIDED FROM HERSELF AND HER FAIR JUDGMENT, WITHOUT THE WHICH WE ARE PICTURES, OR MERE BEASTS.
LAST, AND AS MUCH CONTAINING AS ALL THESE, HER BROTHER IS IN SECRET COME FROM FRANCE; FEEDS ON HIS WONDER, KEEPS HIMSELF IN CLOUDS,

THE OCEAN, OVERPEERING OF HIS LIST, EATS NOT THE FLATS WITH MORE IMPETUOUS HASTE THAN YOUNG LAERTES, IN A RIOTOUS HEAD, O'ERBEARS YOUR OFFICERS.
THE RABBLE CALL HIM LORD, AND, AS THE WORLD WERE NOW BUT TO BEGIN, ANTIQUITY FORGOT, CUSTOM NOT KNOWN, THE RATIFIERS AND PROPS OF EVERY WORD,
THEY CRY 'CHOOSE WE! LAERTES SHALL BE KING!'
CAPS, HANDS, AND TONGUES APPLAUD IT TO THE CLOUDS: 'LAERTES SHALL BE KING, LAERTES KING!'
HOW CHEERFULLY ON THE FALSE TRAIL THEY CRY! O, THIS IS COUNTER, YOU FALSE DANISH DOGS!
BLAM!
RAAAAAH!
THE DOORS ARE BROKE.

WHERE IS THIS KING?
I PRAY YOU, GIVE ME LEAVE.
- SIRS, STAND YOU ALL WITHOUT.
NO, LET'S COME IN.
SCREEE
I THANK YOU. KEEP THE DOOR.
WE WILL, WE WILL.

O THOU VILE KING, GIVE ME MY FATHER!

SHING!

CALMLY, GOOD LAERTES.
TMP

THAT DROP OF BLOOD THAT'S CALM PROCLAIMS ME BASTARD, CRIES CUCKOLD TO MY FATHER,

BRANDS THE HARLOT EVEN HERE BETWEEN THE CHASTE UNSMIRCHED BROW OF MY TRUE MOTHER.
WHAT IS THE CAUSE, LAERTES, THAT THY REBELLION LOOKS SO GIANT-LIKE?

LET HIM GO, GERTRUDE. DO NOT FEAR OUR PERSON.

TELL ME, LAERTES, WHY THOU ART THUS INCENSED.

THERE'S SUCH DIVINITY DOTH HEDGE A KING, THAT TREASON CAN BUT PEEP TO WHAT IT WOULD, ACTS LITTLE OF HIS WILL.

LET HIM GO, GERTRUDE.

SPEAK, MAN.

WHERE IS MY FATHER?

DEAD.

!!

LET HIM DEMAND HIS FILL.
BUT NOT BY HIM.

HOW CAME HE DEAD? I'LL NOT BE JUGGLED WITH.
TO HELL, ALLEGIANCE! VOWS, TO THE BLACKEST DEVIL!

CONSCIENCE AND GRACE, TO THE PROFOUNDEST PIT! I DARE DAMNATION.
TO THIS POINT I STAND, THAT BOTH THE WORLDS I GIVE TO NEGLIGENCE, LET COME WHAT COMES; ONLY I'LL BE REVENGED MOST THOROUGHLY FOR MY FATHER.

MY WILL, NOT ALL THE WORLD.

AND FOR MY MEANS, I'LL HUSBAND THEM SO WELL, THEY SHALL GO FAR WITH LITTLE.

SHUF

GOOD LAERTES, IF YOU DESIRE TO KNOW THE CERTAINTY OF YOUR DEAR FATHER'S DEATH,

IS'T WRIT IN YOUR REVENGE THAT, SWOOPSTAKE, YOU WILL DRAW BOTH FRIEND AND FOE, WINNER AND LOSER?

WILL YOU KNOW THEM THEN?

NONE BUT HIS ENEMIES.

TO HIS GOOD FRIENDS THUS WIDE I'LL OPE MY ARMS; AND LIKE THE KIND LIFE-RENDERING PELICAN, REPAST THEM WITH MY BLOOD.

THAT I AM GUILTLESS OF YOUR FATHER'S DEATH, AND AM MOST SENSIBLE IN GRIEF FOR IT, IT SHALL AS LEVEL TO YOUR JUDGMENT PIERCE AS DAY DOES TO YOUR EYE.

WHY, NOW YOU SPEAK LIKE A GOOD CHILD AND A TRUE GENTLEMAN.

LET HER COME IN.

PAT

HOW NOW! WHAT NOISE IS THAT?

O HEAT, DRY UP MY BRAINS!
TEARS SEVEN TIMES SALT, BURN OUT THE SENSE AND VIRTUE OF MINE EYE!
PAT
PAT
PIT
PIT
BY HEAVEN, THY MADNESS SHALL BE PAID BY WEIGHT, TILL OUR SCALE TURN THE BEAM.
O ROSE OF MAY!
DEAR MAID, KIND SISTER, SWEET OPHELIA!
O HEAVENS! IS'T POSSIBLE, A YOUNG MAID'S WITS SHOULD BE AS MORAL AS AN OLD MAN'S LIFE?

NATURE IS FINE IN LOVE, AND WHERE 'TIS FINE, IT SENDS SOME PRECIOUS INSTANCE OF ITSELF AFTER THE THING IT LOVES.
THEY BORE HIM BAREFACED ON THE BIER; HEY NON NONNY, NONNY, HEY NONNY;
AND IN HIS GRAVE RAIN'D MANY A TEAR -
FARE YOU WELL, MY DOVE!
GRAB!
HADST THOU THY WITS, AND DIDST PERSUADE REVENGE, IT COULD NOT MOVE THUS.
YOU MUST SING A-DOWN A-DOWN,
...

AN YOU CALL HIM A-DOWN-A.
O, HOW THE WHEEL BECOMES IT!
IT IS THE FALSE STEWARD, THAT STOLE HIS MASTER'S DAUGHTER.
THIS NOTHING'S MORE THAN MATTER.
THERE'S ROSEMARY, THAT'S FOR REMEMBRANCE; PRAY, LOVE, REMEMBER.
AND THERE IS PANSIES, THAT'S FOR THOUGHTS.

A DOCUMENT IN MADNESS, THOUGHTS AND REMEMBRANCE FITTED.

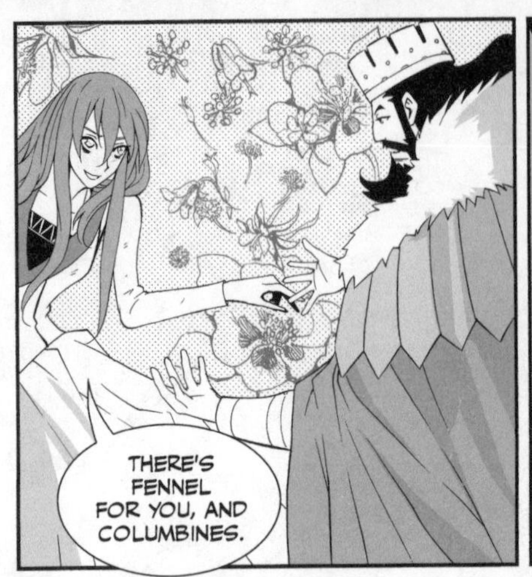
THERE'S FENNEL FOR YOU, AND COLUMBINES.

FLICK

THERE'S RUE FOR YOU;

THERE'S A DAISY.

AND HERE'S SOME FOR ME.

WE MAY CALL IT HERB-GRACE O' SUNDAYS.

O YOU MUST WEAR YOUR RUE WITH A DIFFERENCE.

I WOULD GIVE YOU SOME VIOLETS, BUT THEY WITHERED ALL WHEN MY FATHER DIED.

THEY SAY HE MADE A GOOD END -

THOUGHT AND AFFLICTION, PASSION, HELL ITSELF, SHE TURNS TO FAVOUR AND TO PRETTINESS.

FOR BONNY SWEET ROBIN IS ALL MY JOY.

AND WILL HE NOT COME AGAIN?
AND WILL HE NOT COME AGAIN?
NO, NO, HE IS DEAD,
GO TO THY DEATH-BED,
HE NEVER WILL COME AGAIN.
HIS BEARD WAS AS WHITE AS SNOW,
ALL FLAXEN WAS HIS POLL.
HE IS GONE, HE IS GONE,
AND WE CAST AWAY MOAN.
GOD HA' MERCY ON HIS SOUL!
AND OF ALL CHRISTIAN SOULS, I PRAY GOD.

GOD BE
WI' YE.
DASH

DO YOU SEE THIS, O GOD?

AND THEY SHALL HEAR AND JUDGE 'TWIXT YOU AND ME.

LAERTES, I MUST COMMUNE WITH YOUR GRIEF, OR YOU DENY ME RIGHT. GO BUT APART, MAKE CHOICE OF WHOM YOUR WISEST FRIENDS YOU WILL.

IF BY DIRECT OR BY COLLATERAL HAND THEY FIND US TOUCH'D, WE WILL OUR KINGDOM GIVE, OUR CROWN, OUR LIFE, AND ALL THAT WE CAN OURS, TO YOU IN SATISFACTION;
BUT IF NOT, BE YOU CONTENT TO LEND YOUR PATIENCE TO US, AND WE SHALL JOINTLY LABOUR WITH YOUR SOUL TO GIVE IT DUE CONTENT.

LET THIS BE SO;
HIS MEANS OF DEATH, HIS OBSCURE FUNERAL - NO TROPHY, SWORD, NOR HATCHMENT O'ER HIS BONES, NO NOBLE RITE NOR FORMAL OSTENTATION -
CRY TO BE HEARD, AS 'TWERE FROM HEAVEN TO EARTH, THAT I MUST CALL'T IN QUESTION.
I PRAY YOU, GO WITH ME.
SO YOU SHALL.
AND WHERE THE OFFENCE IS LET THE GREAT AXE FALL.

ACT IV
SCENE VI
ELSEWHERE IN THE CASTLE.
WHAT ARE THEY THAT WOULD SPEAK WITH ME?

SAILORS, SIR. THEY SAY THEY HAVE LETTERS FOR YOU.
LET THEM COME IN.

GOD BLESS YOU, SIR.

LET HIM BLESS THEE TOO.

I DO NOT KNOW FROM WHAT PART OF THE WORLD I SHOULD BE GREETED, IF NOT FROM LORD HAMLET.

HE SHALL, SIR, AN'T PLEASE HIM. THERE'S A LETTER FOR YOU, SIR.
IT COMES FROM THE AMBASSADOR THAT WAS BOUND FOR ENGLAND;
IF YOUR NAME BE HORATIO, AS I AM LET TO KNOW IT IS.
FLAP
CRACK
'HORATIO, WHEN THOU SHALT HAVE OVERLOOKED THIS, GIVE THESE FELLOWS SOME MEANS TO THE KING. THEY HAVE LETTERS FOR HIM.

ERE WE WERE TWO DAYS OLD AT SEA, A PIRATE OF VERY WARLIKE APPOINTMENT GAVE US CHASE.

FINDING OURSELVES TOO SLOW OF SAIL, WE PUT ON A COMPELLED VALOUR, AND IN THE GRAPPLE I BOARDED THEM.

ON THE INSTANT THEY GOT CLEAR OF OUR SHIP, SO I ALONE BECAME THEIR PRISONER.

THEY HAVE DEALT WITH ME LIKE THIEVES OF MERCY. BUT THEY KNEW WHAT THEY DID; I AM TO DO A GOOD TURN FOR THEM.

LET THE KING HAVE THE LETTERS I HAVE SENT, AND REPAIR THOU TO ME WITH AS MUCH SPEED AS THOU WOULDST FLY DEATH.
I HAVE WORDS TO SPEAK IN THINE EAR WILL MAKE THEE DUMB; YET ARE THEY MUCH TOO LIGHT FOR THE BORE OF THE MATTER.
THESE GOOD FELLOWS WILL BRING THEE WHERE I AM.
ROSENCRANTZ AND GUILDENSTERN HOLD THEIR COURSE FOR ENGLAND:
OF THEM I HAVE MUCH TO TELL THEE.
FAREWELL.
'HE THAT THOU KNOWEST THINE, HAMLET.'

FLAP
COME, I WILL MAKE YOU WAY FOR THESE YOUR LETTERS, AND DO'T THE SPEEDIER, THAT YOU MAY DIRECT ME TO HIM FROM WHOM YOU BROUGHT THEM.

NOW MUST YOUR CONSCIENCE MY ACQUAINTANCE SEAL, AND YOU MUST PUT ME IN YOUR HEART FOR FRIEND,

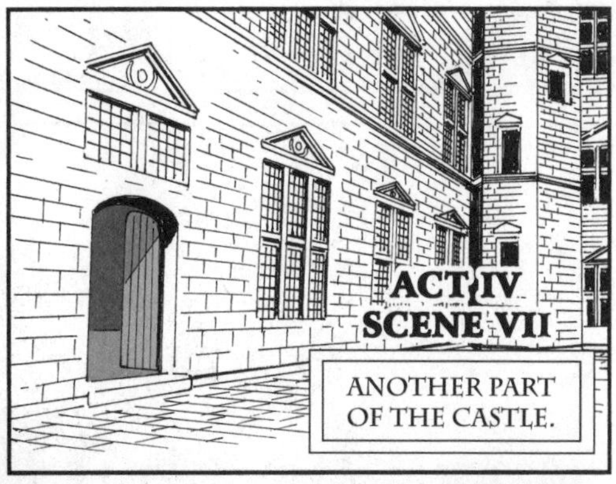
ACT IV
SCENE VII
ANOTHER PART OF THE CASTLE.

SITH YOU HAVE HEARD, AND WITH A KNOWING EAR, THAT HE WHICH HATH YOUR NOBLE FATHER SLAIN PURSUED MY LIFE.

IT WELL APPEARS.
BUT TELL ME WHY YOU PROCEEDED NOT AGAINST THESE FEATS, SO CRIMEFUL AND SO CAPITAL IN NATURE,
AS BY YOUR SAFETY, WISDOM, ALL THINGS ELSE, YOU MAINLY WERE STIRR'D UP.
O, FOR TWO SPECIAL REASONS, WHICH MAY TO YOU, PERHAPS, SEEM MUCH UNSINEW'D, BUT YET TO ME THEY ARE STRONG.
THE QUEEN HIS MOTHER LIVES ALMOST BY HIS LOOKS; AND FOR MYSELF -
MY VIRTUE OR MY PLAGUE, BE IT EITHER WHICH -
SHE'S SO CONJUNCTIVE TO MY LIFE AND SOUL, THAT, AS THE STAR MOVES NOT BUT IN HIS SPHERE, I COULD NOT BUT BY HER.

THE OTHER MOTIVE, WHY TO A PUBLIC COUNT I MIGHT NOT GO, IS THE GREAT LOVE THE GENERAL GENDER BEAR HIM; WHO, DIPPING ALL HIS FAULTS IN THEIR AFFECTION, WOULD, LIKE THE SPRING THAT TURNETH WOOD TO STONE, CONVERT HIS GYVES TO GRACES;

SO THAT MY ARROWS, TOO SLIGHTLY TIMBER'D FOR SO LOUD A WIND, WOULD HAVE REVERTED TO MY BOW AGAIN, AND NOT WHERE I HAD AIM'D THEM.

AND SO HAVE I A NOBLE FATHER LOST, A SISTER DRIVEN INTO DESPERATE TERMS,
THUMP

WHOSE WORTH, IF PRAISES MAY GO BACK AGAIN, STOOD CHALLENGER ON MOUNT OF ALL THE AGE FOR HER PERFECTIONS.

BREAK NOT YOUR SLEEPS FOR THAT. YOU MUST NOT THINK THAT WE ARE MADE OF STUFF SO FLAT AND DULL THAT WE CAN LET OUR BEARD BE SHOOK WITH DANGER AND THINK IT PASTIME.

CLENCH
BUT MY REVENGE WILL COME.

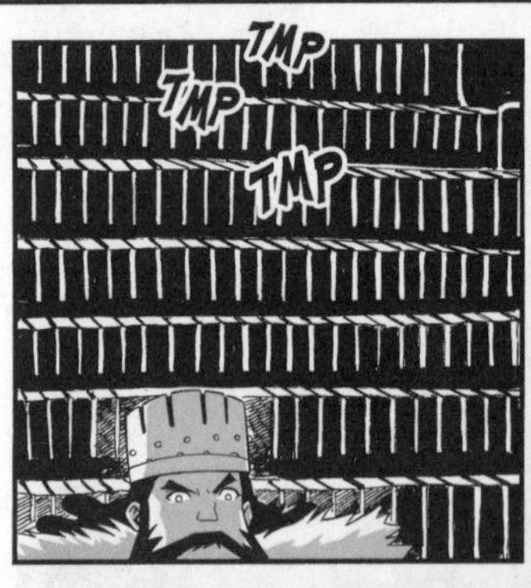
TMP
TMP
TMP

YOU SHORTLY SHALL HEAR MORE.
I LOVED YOUR FATHER, AND WE LOVE OURSELF,
AND THAT, I HOPE, WILL TEACH YOU TO IMAGINE -

LETTERS, MY LORD, FROM HAMLET. THIS TO YOUR MAJESTY; THIS TO THE QUEEN.

HOW NOW! WHAT NEWS?

THEY WERE GIVEN ME BY CLAUDIO. HE RECEIVED THEM OF HIM THAT BROUGHT THEM.

FROM HAMLET! WHO BROUGHT THEM?
SAILORS, MY LORD, THEY SAY; I SAW THEM NOT.

TMP TMP

LAERTES, YOU SHALL HEAR THEM.
LEAVE US.

'HIGH AND MIGHTY, YOU SHALL KNOW I AM SET NAKED ON YOUR KINGDOM.
TO-MORROW SHALL I BEG LEAVE TO SEE YOUR KINGLY EYES.
WHEN I SHALL, FIRST ASKING YOUR PARDON THEREUNTO, RECOUNT THE OCCASION OF MY SUDDEN AND MORE STRANGE RETURN. 'HAMLET.'
KNOW YOU THE HAND?
'TIS HAMLET'S CHARACTER.
'NAKED!' AND IN A POSTSCRIPT HERE, HE SAYS 'ALONE.' CAN YOU ADVISE ME?
WHAT SHOULD THIS MEAN? ARE ALL THE REST COME BACK? OR IS IT SOME ABUSE, AND NO SUCH THING?

I'M LOST IN IT, MY LORD. BUT LET HIM COME;
IT WARMS THE VERY SICKNESS IN MY HEART, THAT I SHALL LIVE AND TELL HIM TO HIS TEETH, 'THUS DIEST THOU.'

IF IT BE SO, LAERTES - AS HOW SHOULD IT BE SO?
HOW OTHERWISE? - WILL YOU BE RULED BY ME?

AY, MY LORD; SO YOU WILL NOT O'ERRULE ME TO A PEACE.

TO THINE OWN PEACE.

IF HE BE NOW RETURN'D, AS CHECKING AT HIS VOYAGE, AND THAT HE MEANS NO MORE TO UNDERTAKE IT, I WILL WORK HIM TO AN EXPLOIT, NOW RIPE IN MY DEVICE, UNDER THE WHICH HE SHALL NOT CHOOSE BUT FALL;

AND FOR HIS DEATH NO WIND OF BLAME SHALL BREATHE, BUT EVEN HIS MOTHER SHALL UNCHARGE THE PRACTICE AND CALL IT ACCIDENT.

IT FALLS RIGHT.
YOU HAVE BEEN TALK'D OF SINCE YOUR TRAVEL MUCH, AND THAT IN HAMLET'S HEARING, FOR A QUALITY WHEREIN, THEY SAY, YOU SHINE.
YOUR SUM OF PARTS DID NOT TOGETHER PLUCK SUCH ENVY FROM HIM AS DID THAT ONE, AND THAT, IN MY REGARD, OF THE UNWORTHIEST SIEGE.
MY LORD, I WILL BE RULED; THE RATHER, IF YOU COULD DEVISE IT SO THAT I MIGHT BE THE ORGAN.
A VERY RIBAND IN THE CAP OF YOUTH, YET NEEDFUL TOO, FOR YOUTH NO LESS BECOMES THE LIGHT AND CARELESS LIVERY THAT IT WEARS
THAN SETTLED AGE HIS SABLES AND HIS WEEDS, IMPORTING HEALTH AND GRAVENESS.
WHAT PART IS THAT, MY LORD?

TWO MONTHS SINCE, HERE WAS A GENTLEMAN OF NORMANDY -

I'VE SEEN MYSELF, AND SERVED AGAINST, THE FRENCH, AND THEY CAN WELL ON HORSEBACK,

BUT THIS GALLANT HAD WITCHCRAFT IN'T. HE GREW UNTO HIS SEAT, AND TO SUCH WONDROUS DOING BROUGHT HIS HORSE, AS HE HAD BEEN INCORPSED AND DEMI-NATURED WITH THE BRAVE BEAST.

SO FAR HE TOPP'D MY THOUGHT, THAT I, IN FORGERY OF SHAPES AND TRICKS, COME SHORT OF WHAT HE DID.

A NORMAN WAS'T?

A NORMAN.

UPON MY LIFE, LAMOND.

THE VERY SAME.

I KNOW HIM WELL; HE IS THE BROOCH INDEED AND GEM OF ALL THE NATION.

HE MADE CONFESSION OF YOU, AND GAVE YOU SUCH A MASTERLY REPORT FOR ART AND EXERCISE IN YOUR DEFENCE, AND FOR YOUR RAPIER MOST ESPECIALLY, THAT HE CRIED OUT 'TWOULD BE A SIGHT INDEED IF ONE COULD MATCH YOU.
THE SCRIMERS OF THEIR NATION, HE SWORE, HAD HAD NEITHER MOTION, GUARD, NOR EYE, IF YOU OPPOSED THEM. SIR, THIS REPORT OF HIS DID HAMLET SO ENVENOM WITH HIS ENVY THAT HE COULD NOTHING DO BUT WISH AND BEG YOUR SUDDEN COMING O'ER, TO PLAY WITH HIM.
NOW, OUT OF THIS -

LAERTES, WAS YOUR FATHER DEAR TO YOU?
OR ARE YOU LIKE THE PAINTING OF A SORROW, A FACE WITHOUT A HEART?

WHAT OUT OF THIS, MY LORD?

NOT THAT I THINK YOU DID NOT LOVE YOUR FATHER, BUT THAT I KNOW LOVE IS BEGUN BY TIME, AND THAT I SEE, IN PASSAGES OF PROOF, TIME QUALIFIES THE SPARK AND FIRE OF IT.

WHY ASK YOU THIS?

THERE LIVES WITHIN THE VERY FLAME OF LOVE A KIND OF WICK OR SNUFF THAT WILL ABATE IT; AND NOTHING IS AT A LIKE GOODNESS STILL,
FOR GOODNESS, GROWING TO A PLEURISY, DIES IN HIS OWN TOO MUCH. THAT WE WOULD DO WE SHOULD DO WHEN WE WOULD; FOR THIS 'WOULD' CHANGES, AND HATH ABATEMENTS AND DELAYS AS MANY AS THERE ARE TONGUES, ARE HANDS, ARE ACCIDENTS;

AND THEN THIS 'SHOULD' IS LIKE A SPENDTHRIFT SIGH THAT HURTS BY EASING.

BUT, TO THE QUICK O' THE ULCER:

HAMLET COMES BACK: WHAT WOULD YOU UNDERTAKE TO SHOW YOURSELF YOUR FATHER'S SON IN DEED MORE THAN IN WORDS?

TO CUT HIS THROAT I' THE CHURCH.

BUT, GOOD LAERTES, WILL YOU DO THIS, KEEP CLOSE WITHIN YOUR CHAMBER. HAMLET RETURN'D SHALL KNOW YOU ARE COME HOME:

WE'LL PUT ON THOSE SHALL PRAISE YOUR EXCELLENCE, AND SET A DOUBLE VARNISH ON THE FAME THE FRENCHMAN GAVE YOU, BRING YOU IN FINE TOGETHER AND WAGER ON YOUR HEADS.

HE, BEING REMISS, MOST GENEROUS AND FREE FROM ALL CONTRIVING, WILL NOT PERUSE THE FOILS;

SO THAT, WITH EASE, OR WITH A LITTLE SHUFFLING, YOU MAY CHOOSE A SWORD UNBATED, AND IN A PASS OF PRACTICE, REQUITE HIM FOR YOUR FATHER.

I WILL DO'T.
AND, FOR THAT PURPOSE, I'LL ANOINT MY SWORD. I BOUGHT AN UNCTION OF A MOUNTEBANK, SO MORTAL THAT, BUT DIP A KNIFE IN IT, WHERE IT DRAWS BLOOD NO CATAPLASM SO RARE, COLLECTED FROM ALL SIMPLES THAT HAVE VIRTUE UNDER THE MOON, CAN SAVE THE THING FROM DEATH THAT IS BUT SCRATCH'D WITHAL.
I'LL TOUCH MY POINT WITH THIS CONTAGION, THAT, IF I GALL HIM SLIGHTLY, IT MAY BE DEATH.
LET'S FURTHER THINK OF THIS, WEIGH WHAT CONVENIENCE BOTH OF TIME AND MEANS MAY FIT US TO OUR SHAPE.
IF THIS SHOULD FAIL, AND THAT OUR DRIFT LOOK THROUGH OUR BAD PERFORMANCE, 'TWERE BETTER NOT ASSAY'D.
THEREFORE THIS PROJECT SHOULD HAVE A BACK OR SECOND, THAT MIGHT HOLD, IF THIS SHOULD BLAST IN PROOF.
SOFT! LET ME SEE.
WE'LL MAKE A SOLEMN WAGER ON YOUR CUNNINGS -

WHEN IN YOUR MOTION YOU ARE HOT AND DRY -
AS MAKE YOUR BOUTS MORE VIOLENT TO THAT END - AND THAT HE CALLS FOR DRINK, I'LL HAVE PREPARED HIM A CHALICE FOR THE NONCE;
WHEREON BUT SIPPING, IF HE BY CHANCE ESCAPE YOUR VENOM'D STUCK, OUR PURPOSE MAY HOLD THERE.
I HA'T!
BUT STAY, WHAT NOISE?
STEP...
STEP...

TMP
TMP
TMP

HOW NOW, SWEET QUEEN!
ONE WOE DOTH TREAD UPON ANOTHER'S HEEL, SO FAST THEY FOLLOW;

DROWN'D!

O, WHERE?

THERE IS A WILLOW GROWS ASLANT A BROOK, THAT SHOWS HIS HOAR LEAVES IN THE GLASSY STREAM.
THERE WITH FANTASTIC GARLANDS DID SHE COME OF CROW-FLOWERS, NETTLES, DAISIES, AND LONG PURPLES, THAT LIBERAL SHEPHERDS GIVE A GROSSER NAME,
BUT OUR COLD MAIDS DO DEAD MEN'S FINGERS CALL THEM.
THERE ON THE PENDENT BOUGHS HER CORONET WEEDS CLAMBERING TO HANG,
CRACK-
SPLASH!
AN ENVIOUS SLIVER BROKE,
WHEN DOWN HER WEEDY TROPHIES AND HERSELF FELL IN THE WEEPING BROOK.

HER CLOTHES SPREAD WIDE, AND, MERMAID-LIKE, AWHILE THEY BORE HER UP: WHICH TIME SHE CHANTED SNATCHES OF OLD TUNES, AS ONE INCAPABLE OF HER OWN DISTRESS, OR LIKE A CREATURE NATIVE AND INDUED UNTO THAT ELEMENT.
BUT LONG IT COULD NOT BE TILL THAT HER GARMENTS, HEAVY WITH THEIR DRINK, PULL'D THE POOR WRETCH FROM HER MELODIOUS LAY TO MUDDY DEATH.
ALAS, THEN, SHE IS DROWN'D?
DROWN'D, DROWN'D.

WHEN THESE ARE GONE, THE WOMAN WILL BE OUT.
ADIEU, MY LORD; I HAVE A SPEECH OF FIRE, THAT FAIN WOULD BLAZE, BUT THAT THIS FOLLY DOUTS IT.

TOO MUCH OF WATER HAST THOU, POOR OPHELIA, AND THEREFORE I FORBID MY TEARS.
BUT YET IT IS OUR TRICK; NATURE HER CUSTOM HOLDS, LET SHAME SAY WHAT IT WILL.

ACT V
SCENE I
LET'S FOLLOW, GERTRUDE; HOW MUCH I HAD TO DO TO CALM HIS RAGE! NOW FEAR I THIS WILL GIVE IT START AGAIN; THEREFORE LET'S FOLLOW.

A CHURCHYARD

IS SHE TO BE BURIED IN CHRISTIAN BURIAL,

TCHUNK

TCHUNK

WHEN SHE WILFULLY SEEKS HER OWN SALVATION?

I TELL THEE SHE IS, AND THEREFORE MAKE HER GRAVE STRAIGHT.

TCHUNK

THE CROWNER HATH SAT ON HER, AND FINDS IT CHRISTIAN BURIAL.
TCH-

HOW CAN THAT BE, UNLESS SHE DROWNED HERSELF IN HER OWN DEFENCE?

WHY, 'TIS FOUND SO.

TCHUNK!
AND AN ACT HATH THREE BRANCHES. IT IS TO ACT, TO DO, TO PERFORM: ARGAL, SHE DROWNED HERSELF WITTINGLY.
TCHUNK!
IT MUST BE 'SE OFFENDENDO', IT CANNOT BE ELSE.
FOR HERE LIES THE POINT: IF I DROWN MYSELF WITTINGLY, IT ARGUES AN ACT:
NAY, BUT HEAR YOU, GOODMAN DELVER -
GIVE ME LEAVE. HERE LIES THE WATER; GOOD. HERE STANDS THE MAN; GOOD.
IF THE MAN GO TO THIS WATER, AND DROWN HIMSELF, IT IS, WILL HE, NILL HE, HE GOES -
- MARK YOU THAT.
BUT IF THE WATER COME TO HIM AND DROWN HIM, HE DROWNS NOT HIMSELF.
ARGAL, HE THAT IS NOT GUILTY OF HIS OWN DEATH SHORTENS NOT HIS OWN LIFE.

WILL YOU HA' THE TRUTH ON'T? IF THIS HAD NOT BEEN A GENTLEWOMAN, SHE SHOULD HAVE BEEN BURIED OUT O' CHRISTIAN BURIAL.

BUT IS THIS LAW?
AY, MARRY, IS'T, CROWNER'S QUEST LAW.

WHY, THERE THOU SAY'ST. AND THE MORE PITY THAT GREAT FOLK SHOULD HAVE COUNTENANCE IN THIS WORLD TO DROWN OR HANG THEMSELVES, MORE THAN THEIR EVEN CHRISTIAN.

WAS HE A GENTLEMAN?

COME, MY SPADE. THERE IS NO ANCIENT GENTLEMAN BUT GARDENERS, DITCHERS, AND GRAVE-MAKERS: THEY HOLD UP ADAM'S PROFESSION.
SHFF

HE WAS THE FIRST THAT EVER BORE ARMS.

WHY, HE HAD NONE.

SHFF
WHAT, ART A HEATHEN? HOW DOST THOU UNDERSTAND THE SCRIPTURE? THE SCRIPTURE SAYS 'ADAM DIGGED'. COULD HE DIG WITHOUT ARMS?
I'LL PUT ANOTHER QUESTION TO THEE. IF THOU ANSWEREST ME NOT TO THE PURPOSE, CONFESS THYSELF -
GO TO.
WHAT IS HE THAT BUILDS STRONGER THAN EITHER THE MASON, THE SHIPWRIGHT, OR THE CARPENTER?
THE GALLOWS-MAKER; FOR THAT FRAME OUTLIVES A THOUSAND TENANTS.
I LIKE THY WIT WELL, IN GOOD FAITH. THE GALLOWS DOES WELL. BUT HOW DOES IT WELL?
HA!

IT DOES WELL TO THOSE THAT DO ILL.
NOW THOU DOST ILL TO SAY THE GALLOWS IS BUILT STRONGER THAN THE CHURCH; ARGAL, THE GALLOWS MAY DO WELL TO THEE.

'WHO BUILDS STRONGER THAN A MASON, A SHIPWRIGHT, OR A CARPENTER?'
AY, TELL ME THAT, AND UNYOKE.

MARRY, NOW I CAN TELL.

TO'T.
MASS, I CANNOT TELL.

CUDGEL THY BRAINS NO MORE ABOUT IT, FOR YOUR DULL ASS WILL NOT MEND HIS PACE WITH BEATING;
AND, WHEN YOU ARE ASKED THIS QUESTION NEXT, SAY 'A GRAVE-MAKER'.
SHFF
TCHUNK
THE HOUSES THAT HE MAKES LAST TILL DOOMSDAY. GO, GET THEE TO YAUGHAN;
FETCH ME A STOUP OF LIQUOR
SHFF
IN YOUTH, WHEN I DID LOVE, DID LOVE, METHOUGHT IT WAS VERY SWEET, TO CONTRACT, O, THE TIME, FOR, AH, MY BEHOVE, O, METHOUGHT, THERE WAS NOTHING MEET.
SHFF
TCHUNK

CUSTOM HATH MADE IT IN HIM A PROPERTY OF EASINESS.
'TIS E'EN SO; THE HAND OF LITTLE EMPLOYMENT HATH THE DAINTIER SENSE.

HAS THIS FELLOW NO FEELING OF HIS BUSINESS, THAT HE SINGS AT GRAVE-MAKING?

SHFF!

BUT AGE, WITH HIS STEALING STEPS, HATH CLAW'D ME IN HIS CLUTCH,

AND HATH SHIPPED ME INTO THE LAND, AS IF I HAD NEVER BEEN SUCH.

ROLL
ROLL
THUNK

ROLLLLL...

THAT SKULL HAD A TONGUE IN IT, AND COULD SING ONCE. HOW THE KNAVE JOWLS IT TO THE GROUND, AS IF IT WERE CAIN'S JAW-BONE, THAT DID THE FIRST MURDER!
IT MIGHT BE THE PATE OF A POLITICIAN, WHICH THIS ASS NOW O'ER-REACHES; ONE THAT WOULD CIRCUMVENT GOD, MIGHT IT NOT?
IT MIGHT, MY LORD.
OR OF A COURTIER, WHICH COULD SAY 'GOOD MORROW, SWEET LORD! HOW DOST THOU, GOOD LORD?' THIS MIGHT BE MY LORD SUCH-A-ONE, THAT PRAISED MY LORD SUCH-A-ONE'S HORSE WHEN HE MEANT TO BEG IT, MIGHT IT NOT?
AY, MY LORD.
WHY, E'EN SO: AND NOW MY LADY WORM'S; CHAPLESS, AND KNOCKED ABOUT THE MAZZARD WITH A SEXTON'S SPADE.
HERE'S FINE REVOLUTION,
AN WE HAD THE TRICK TO SEE'T.
DID THESE BONES COST NO MORE THE BREEDING BUT TO PLAY AT LOGGATS WITH 'EM?
MINE ACHE TO THINK ON'T.

O,
A PIT OF CLAY
FOR TO BE
MADE FOR SUCH
A GUEST IS
MEET.

A PICK-AXE,
AND A SPADE,
A SPADE, FOR AND
A SHROUDING
SHEET:

BONK
BONK
BONK
SHFF
THOK!

THERE'S ANOTHER: WHY MAY NOT THAT BE THE SKULL OF A LAWYER? WHERE BE HIS QUIDDITIES NOW, HIS QUILLETS, HIS CASES, HIS TENURES, AND HIS TRICKS?
WHY DOES HE SUFFER THIS RUDE KNAVE NOW TO KNOCK HIM ABOUT THE SCONCE WITH A DIRTY SHOVEL, AND WILL NOT TELL HIM OF HIS ACTION OF BATTERY?
HUM! THIS FELLOW MIGHT BE IN'S TIME A GREAT BUYER OF LAND, WITH HIS STATUTES, HIS RECOGNIZANCES, HIS FINES, HIS DOUBLE VOUCHERS, HIS RECOVERIES.
IS THIS THE FINE OF HIS FINES, AND THE RECOVERY OF HIS RECOVERIES, TO HAVE HIS FINE PATE FULL OF FINE DIRT?
WILL HIS VOUCHERS VOUCH HIM NO MORE OF HIS PURCHASES, AND DOUBLE ONES TOO, THAN THE LENGTH AND BREADTH OF A PAIR OF INDENTURES?
THE VERY CONVEYANCES OF HIS LANDS WILL HARDLY LIE IN THIS BOX; AND MUST THE INHERITOR HIMSELF HAVE NO MORE, HA?

IS NOT PARCHMENT MADE OF SHEEP-SKINS?
NOT A JOT MORE, MY LORD.

I WILL SPEAK TO THIS FELLOW.
RUSTLE-

AY, MY LORD, AND OF CALF-SKINS TOO.
THEY ARE SHEEP AND CALVES WHICH SEEK OUT ASSURANCE IN THAT.

WHOSE GRAVE'S THIS, SIRRAH?

SHFF
O, A PIT OF CLAY FOR TO BE MADE FOR SUCH A GUEST IS MEET.
MINE, SIR.

I THINK IT BE THINE, INDEED; FOR THOU LIEST IN'T.

YOU LIE OUT ON'T, SIR, AND THEREFORE IT IS NOT YOURS. FOR MY PART, I DO NOT LIE IN'T, AND YET IT IS MINE.
TCHUNK!

THOU DOST LIE IN'T, TO BE IN'T AND SAY IT IS THINE. 'TIS FOR THE DEAD, NOT FOR THE QUICK; THEREFORE THOU LIEST.

SHFF
VWIP!
'TIS A QUICK LIE, SIR; 'T WILL AWAY AGAIN FROM ME TO YOU.
WHAT WOMAN, THEN?
WHAT MAN DOST THOU DIG IT FOR?
FOR NO MAN, SIR.
FOR NONE, NEITHER.
WHO IS TO BE BURIED IN'T?

ONE THAT WAS A WOMAN, SIR; BUT, REST HER SOUL, SHE'S DEAD.
TCHUNK

HOW ABSOLUTE THE KNAVE IS! WE MUST SPEAK BY THE CARD, OR EQUIVOCATION WILL UNDO US.
BY THE LORD, HORATIO, THESE THREE YEARS I HAVE TAKEN A NOTE OF IT;

HOW LONG HAST THOU BEEN A GRAVE-MAKER?
THE AGE IS GROWN SO PICKED THAT THE TOE OF THE PEASANT COMES SO NEAR THE HEEL OF THE COURTIER, HE GALLS HIS KIBE.

HOW LONG IS THAT SINCE?
OF ALL THE DAYS I' THE YEAR, I CAME TO'T THAT DAY THAT OUR LAST KING HAMLET OVERCAME FORTINBRAS.
SHFF
CANNOT YOU TELL THAT? EVERY FOOL CAN TELL THAT. IT WAS THE VERY DAY THAT YOUNG HAMLET WAS BORN - HE THAT IS MAD, AND SENT INTO ENGLAND.
AY, MARRY, WHY WAS HE SENT INTO ENGLAND?
WHY, BECAUSE HE WAS MAD; HE SHALL RECOVER HIS WITS THERE; OR, IF HE DO NOT, IT'S NO GREAT MATTER THERE.
WHY?

'TWILL NOT BE SEEN IN HIM THERE; THERE THE MEN ARE AS MAD AS HE.
FAITH, E'EN WITH LOSING HIS WITS.
HOW STRANGELY?
VERY STRANGELY, THEY SAY.
HOW CAME HE MAD?
UPON WHAT GROUND?
WHY, HERE IN DENMARK. I HAVE BEEN SEXTON HERE, MAN AND BOY, THIRTY YEARS.
HOW LONG WILL A MAN LIE I' THE EARTH ERE HE ROT?

WHY HE MORE THAN ANOTHER?

I' FAITH, IF HE BE NOT ROTTEN BEFORE HE DIE - AS WE HAVE MANY POCKY CORSES NOW-A-DAYS THAT WILL SCARCE HOLD THE LAYING IN - HE WILL LAST YOU SOME EIGHT YEAR OR NINE YEAR. A TANNER WILL LAST YOU NINE YEAR.
WHY, SIR, HIS HIDE IS SO TANNED WITH HIS TRADE THAT HE WILL KEEP OUT WATER A GREAT WHILE. AND YOUR WATER IS A SORE DECAYER OF YOUR WHORESON DEAD BODY.

HERE'S A SKULL NOW; THIS SKULL HAS LAIN IN THE EARTH THREE AND TWENTY YEARS.

WHOSE DO YOU THINK IT WAS?
A WHORESON MAD FELLOW'S IT WAS.

WHOSE WAS IT?

A PESTILENCE ON HIM FOR A MAD ROGUE! A' POURED A FLAGON OF RHENISH ON MY HEAD ONCE.
CHUNK
NAY, I KNOW NOT.

THIS?

E'EN THAT.
TUNK

THIS SAME SKULL, SIR, WAS YORICK'S SKULL, THE KING'S JESTER.

TOSS

LET ME SEE.

TUNK

ALAS, POOR YORICK!

I KNEW HIM, HORATIO: A FELLOW OF INFINITE JEST, OF MOST EXCELLENT FANCY.
HE HATH BORNE ME ON HIS BACK A THOUSAND TIMES; AND NOW, HOW ABHORRED IN MY IMAGINATION IT IS!
MY GORGE RISES AT IT.

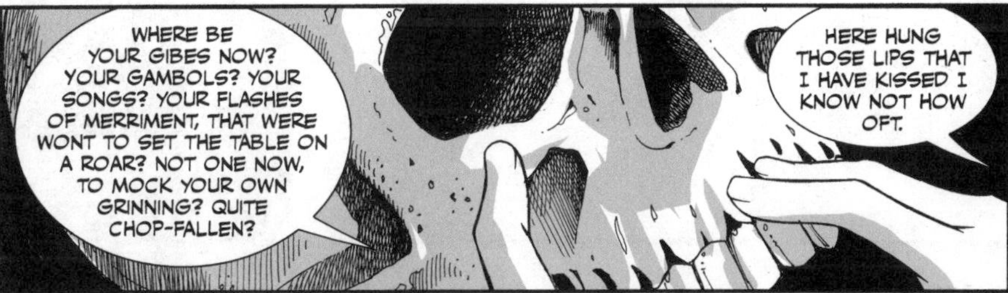
HERE HUNG THOSE LIPS THAT I HAVE KISSED I KNOW NOT HOW OFT.
WHERE BE YOUR GIBES NOW? YOUR GAMBOLS? YOUR SONGS? YOUR FLASHES OF MERRIMENT, THAT WERE WONT TO SET THE TABLE ON A ROAR? NOT ONE NOW, TO MOCK YOUR OWN GRINNING? QUITE CHOP-FALLEN?

NOW GET YOU TO MY LADY'S CHAMBER, AND TELL HER, LET HER PAINT AN INCH THICK, TO THIS FAVOUR SHE MUST COME. MAKE HER LAUGH AT THAT.

PRITHEE, HORATIO, TELL ME ONE THING.
WHAT'S THAT, MY LORD?

DOST THOU THINK ALEXANDER LOOKED O' THIS FASHION I' THE EARTH?

E'EN SO.
AND SMELT SO? PAH!
TO WHAT BASE USES WE MAY RETURN, HORATIO!
E'EN SO, MY LORD.
WHY MAY NOT IMAGINATION TRACE THE NOBLE DUST OF ALEXANDER TILL HE FIND IT STOPPING A BUNG-HOLE?

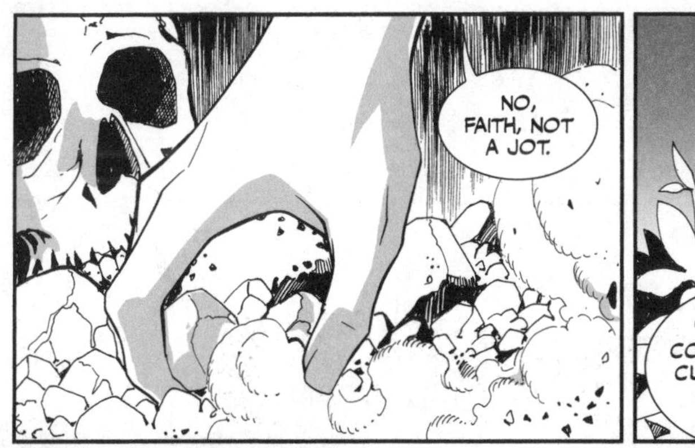
NO, FAITH, NOT A JOT.

'TWERE TO CONSIDER TOO CURIOUSLY TO CONSIDER SO.

BUT TO FOLLOW HIM THITHER WITH MODESTY ENOUGH, AND LIKELIHOOD TO LEAD IT, AS THUS: ALEXANDER DIED, ALEXANDER WAS BURIED, ALEXANDER RETURNETH INTO DUST; THE DUST IS EARTH; OF EARTH WE MAKE LOAM;
AND WHY OF THAT LOAM, WHERETO HE WAS CONVERTED, MIGHT THEY NOT STOP A BEER-BARREL?
CRUMBLE...

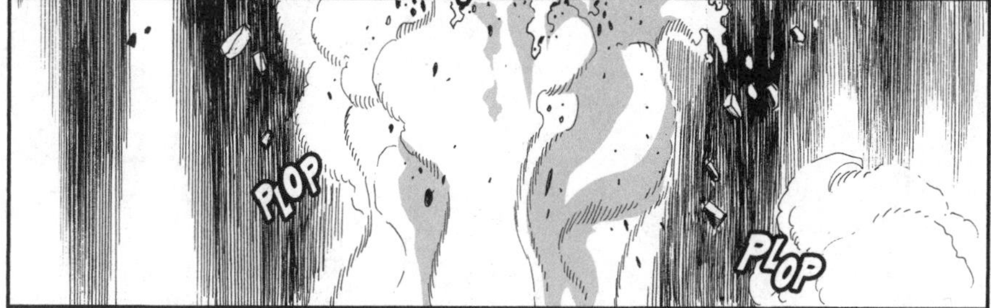
PLOP
PLOP

IMPERIOUS CAESAR, DEAD AND TURN'D TO CLAY, MIGHT STOP A HOLE TO KEEP THE WIND AWAY. O, THAT THAT EARTH, WHICH KEPT THE WORLD IN AWE, SHOULD PATCH A WALL TO EXPEL THE WINTER'S FLAW!

FLUMP

HERE COMES THE KING. THE QUEEN, THE COURTIERS: WHO IS THIS THEY FOLLOW? AND WITH SUCH MAIMED RITES? THIS DOTH BETOKEN THE CORSE THEY FOLLOW DID WITH DESPERATE HAND FORDO ITS OWN LIFE.

'TWAS OF SOME ESTATE. COUCH WE AWHILE AND MARK.

WHAT CEREMONY ELSE?
HER OBSEQUIES HAVE BEEN AS FAR ENLARGED AS WE HAVE WARRANTIES.
HER DEATH WAS DOUBTFUL; AND, BUT THAT GREAT COMMAND O'ERSWAYS THE ORDER, SHE SHOULD IN GROUND UNSANCTIFIED HAVE LODGED TILL THE LAST TRUMPET.
THAT IS LAERTES, A VERY NOBLE YOUTH: MARK.
WHAT CEREMONY ELSE?

MUST THERE NO MORE BE DONE?

FOR CHARITABLE PRAYERS, SHARDS, FLINTS AND PEBBLES SHOULD BE THROWN ON HER.
YET HERE SHE IS ALLOW'D HER VIRGIN RITES, HER MAIDEN STREWMENTS, AND THE BRINGING HOME OF BELL AND BURIAL.

NO MORE BE DONE. WE SHOULD PROFANE THE SERVICE OF THE DEAD TO SING A REQUIEM AND SUCH REST TO HER AS TO PEACE-PARTED SOULS.

LAY HER I' THE EARTH, AND FROM HER FAIR AND UNPOLLUTED FLESH MAY VIOLETS SPRING!

I TELL THEE, CHURLISH PRIEST, A MINISTERING ANGEL SHALL MY SISTER BE WHEN THOU LIEST HOWLING.

WHAT, THE FAIR OPHELIA?

SWEETS TO THE SWEET. FAREWELL!

I HOPED THOU SHOULDST HAVE BEEN MY HAMLET'S WIFE;
I THOUGHT THY BRIDE-BED TO HAVE DECK'D, SWEET MAID, AND NOT HAVE STREW'D THY GRAVE.
TCHUNK...
O, TREBLE WOE FALL TEN TIMES TREBLE ON THAT CURSED HEAD, WHOSE WICKED DEED THY MOST INGENIOUS SENSE DEPRIVED THEE OF!
HOLD OFF THE EARTH AWHILE, TILL I HAVE CAUGHT HER ONCE MORE IN MINE ARMS.
THOK!

NOW PILE YOUR DUST UPON THE QUICK AND DEAD, TILL OF THIS FLAT A MOUNTAIN YOU HAVE MADE, TO O'ERTOP OLD PELION, OR THE SKYISH HEAD OF BLUE OLYMPUS.
THUMP
SHUF
WHAT IS HE WHOSE GRIEF BEARS SUCH AN EMPHASIS? WHOSE PHRASE OF SORROW CONJURES THE WANDERING STARS, AND MAKES THEM STAND LIKE WONDER-WOUNDED HEARERS?

FLAP-
THIS IS I, HAMLET THE DANE.
RRRRRGH!

GRAB
THE DEVIL TAKE THY SOUL!
THOU PRAY'ST NOT WELL.
I PRITHEE, TAKE THY FINGERS FROM MY THROAT;
FOR, THOUGH I AM NOT SPLENATIVE AND RASH, YET HAVE I SOMETHING IN ME DANGEROUS,
WHICH LET THY WISENESS FEAR. AWAY THY HAND!
GH!
WHUMP
HAMLET! HAMLET!
PLUCK THEM ASUNDER.
GENTLEMEN -
GOOD MY LORD, BE QUIET.

HUFF
HUFF
WHY, I WILL FIGHT WITH HIM UPON THIS THEME UNTIL MY EYELIDS WILL NO LONGER WAG.
O MY SON, WHAT THEME?
I LOVED OPHELIA; FORTY THOUSAND BROTHERS COULD NOT, WITH ALL THEIR QUANTITY OF LOVE, MAKE UP MY SUM. WHAT WILT THOU DO FOR HER?

O, HE IS MAD, LAERTES.

RRRGH!!

FOR LOVE OF GOD, FORBEAR HIM!

'SWOUNDS, SHOW ME WHAT THOU'LT DO:
WOUL'T WEEP? WOUL'T FIGHT? WOUL'T FAST? WOUL'T TEAR THYSELF? WOUL'T DRINK UP EISEL? EAT A CROCODILE? I'LL DO'T.

AND IF THOU PRATE OF MOUNTAINS, LET THEM THROW MILLIONS OF ACRES ON US, TILL OUR GROUND, SINGEING HIS PATE AGAINST THE BURNING ZONE, MAKE OSSA LIKE A WART!
DOST THOU COME HERE TO WHINE? TO OUTFACE ME WITH LEAPING IN HER GRAVE? BE BURIED QUICK WITH HER, AND SO WILL I.
NAY, AN THOU'LT MOUTH, I'LL RANT AS WELL AS THOU.
THIS IS MERE MADNESS: AND THUS AWHILE THE FIT WILL WORK ON HIM;
ANON, AS PATIENT AS THE FEMALE DOVE, WHEN THAT HER GOLDEN COUPLETS ARE DISCLOSED, HIS SILENCE WILL SIT DROOPING.

PAT
PAT
PAT
HEAR YOU, SIR; WHAT IS THE REASON THAT YOU USE ME THUS? I LOVED YOU EVER.
I PRAY YOU, GOOD HORATIO, WAIT UPON HIM.
BUT IT IS NO MATTER. LET HERCULES HIMSELF DO WHAT HE MAY, THE CAT WILL MEW AND DOG WILL HAVE HIS DAY.
CLENCH –

...

STRENGTHEN YOUR PATIENCE IN OUR LAST NIGHT'S SPEECH; WE'LL PUT THE MATTER TO THE PRESENT PUSH.

GOOD GERTRUDE, SET SOME WATCH OVER YOUR SON. THIS GRAVE SHALL HAVE A LIVING MONUMENT. AN HOUR OF QUIET SHORTLY SHALL WE SEE;
TILL THEN, IN PATIENCE OUR PROCEEDING BE.

ELSINORE.
THE CASTLE.

ACT V
SCENE II

NOW SHALL YOU SEE THE OTHER; YOU DO REMEMBER ALL THE CIRCUMSTANCE?

SO MUCH FOR THIS, SIR.

REMEMBER IT, MY LORD!
SIR, IN MY HEART THERE WAS A KIND OF FIGHTING, THAT WOULD NOT LET ME SLEEP. METHOUGHT I LAY WORSE THAN THE MUTINIES IN THE BILBOES.

AND THAT SHOULD TEACH US THERE'S A DIVINITY THAT SHAPES OUR ENDS, ROUGH-HEW THEM HOW WE WILL -

THAT IS MOST CERTAIN.

RASHLY, AND PRAISED BE RASHNESS FOR IT, LET US KNOW, OUR INDISCRETION SOMETIMES SERVES US WELL, WHEN OUR DEEP PLOTS DO PALL;

UP FROM MY CABIN,

MY SEA-GOWN SCARF'D ABOUT ME, IN THE DARK GROPED I TO FIND OUT THEM; HAD MY DESIRE. FINGER'D THEIR PACKET, AND IN FINE WITHDREW TO MINE OWN ROOM AGAIN,

MAKING SO BOLD, MY FEARS FORGETTING MANNERS, TO UNSEAL THEIR GRAND COMMISSION;
WHERE I FOUND, HORATIO - O ROYAL KNAVERY! - AN EXACT COMMAND, LARDED WITH MANY SEVERAL SORTS OF REASONS, IMPORTING DENMARK'S HEALTH AND ENGLAND'S TOO, WITH, HO!
SUCH BUGS AND GOBLINS IN MY LIFE,
THAT, ON THE SUPERVISE, NO LEISURE BATED, NO, NOT TO STAY THE GRINDING OF THE AXE, MY HEAD SHOULD BE STRUCK OFF.
CRUMPLE
HERE'S THE COMMISSION: READ IT AT MORE LEISURE. BUT WILT THOU HEAR ME HOW I DID PROCEED?
I BESEECH YOU.
IS'T POSSIBLE?

BEING THUS BE-NETTED ROUND WITH VILLANIES - ERE I COULD MAKE A PROLOGUE TO MY BRAINS, THEY HAD BEGUN THE PLAY - I SAT ME DOWN, DEVISED A NEW COMMISSION, WROTE IT FAIR:
I ONCE DID HOLD IT, AS OUR STATISTS DO, A BASENESS TO WRITE FAIR, AND LABOUR'D MUCH HOW TO FORGET THAT LEARNING; BUT, SIR, NOW IT DID ME YEOMAN'S SERVICE.
WILT THOU KNOW THE EFFECT OF WHAT I WROTE?
AY, GOOD MY LORD.

AN EARNEST CONJURATION FROM THE KING, AS ENGLAND WAS HIS FAITHFUL TRIBUTARY,
AS LOVE BETWEEN THEM LIKE THE PALM MIGHT FLOURISH, AS PEACE SHOULD STIFF HER WHEATEN GARLAND WEAR AND STAND A COMMA 'TWEEN THEIR AMITIES, AND MANY SUCH-LIKE 'AS'ES OF GREAT CHARGE,
THAT, ON THE VIEW AND KNOWING OF THESE CONTENTS, WITHOUT DEBATEMENT FURTHER, MORE OR LESS, HE SHOULD THE BEARERS PUT TO SUDDEN DEATH, NOT SHRIVING-TIME ALLOW'D.
HOW WAS THIS SEAL'D?
WHY, EVEN IN THAT WAS HEAVEN ORDINANT. I HAD MY FATHER'S SIGNET IN MY PURSE, WHICH WAS THE MODEL OF THAT DANISH SEAL;
FOLDED THE WRIT UP IN FORM OF THE OTHER, SUBSCRIBED IT, GAVE'T THE IMPRESSION, PLACED IT SAFELY, THE CHANGELING NEVER KNOWN.
NOW, THE NEXT DAY WAS OUR SEA-FIGHT; AND WHAT TO THIS WAS SEQUENT THOU KNOW'ST ALREADY.

SO GUILDENSTERN AND ROSENCRANTZ GO TO'T.
WHY, MAN, THEY DID MAKE LOVE TO THIS EMPLOYMENT.
THEY ARE NOT NEAR MY CONSCIENCE; THEIR DEFEAT DOES BY THEIR OWN INSINUATION GROW.
'TIS DANGEROUS WHEN THE BASER NATURE COMES BETWEEN THE PASS AND FELL INCENSED POINTS OF MIGHTY OPPOSITES.
DOES IT NOT, THINK'ST THEE, STAND ME NOW UPON -
WHY, WHAT A KING IS THIS!
HE THAT HATH KILL'D MY KING AND WHORED MY MOTHER, POPP'D IN BETWEEN THE ELECTION AND MY HOPES, THROWN OUT HIS ANGLE FOR MY PROPER LIFE, AND WITH SUCH COZENAGE -
IS'T NOT PERFECT CONSCIENCE TO QUIT HIM WITH THIS ARM?
AND IS'T NOT TO BE DAMN'D TO LET THIS CANKER OF OUR NATURE COME IN FURTHER EVIL?

AND A MAN'S LIFE'S NO MORE THAN TO SAY 'ONE.'
IT MUST BE SHORTLY KNOWN TO HIM FROM ENGLAND WHAT IS THE ISSUE OF THE BUSINESS THERE.
IT WILL BE SHORT. THE INTERIM IS MINE;

BUT I AM VERY SORRY, GOOD HORATIO, THAT TO LAERTES I FORGOT MYSELF; FOR, BY THE IMAGE OF MY CAUSE, I SEE THE PORTRAITURE OF HIS.
I'LL COURT HIS FAVOURS.

BUT SURE THE BRAVERY OF HIS GRIEF DID PUT ME INTO A TOWERING PASSION.

HM?
PEACE! WHO COMES HERE?
YOUR LORDSHIP IS RIGHT WELCOME BACK TO DENMARK.
I HUMBLY THANK YOU, SIR.

NO, MY GOOD LORD.

DOST KNOW THIS WATER-FLY?

OSRIC

'TIS A CHOUGH; BUT, AS I SAY, SPACIOUS IN THE POSSESSION OF DIRT.

THY STATE IS THE MORE GRACIOUS; FOR 'TIS A VICE TO KNOW HIM. HE HATH MUCH LAND, AND FERTILE; LET A BEAST BE LORD OF BEASTS, AND HIS CRIB SHALL STAND AT THE KING'S MESS;

SWEET LORD, IF YOUR LORDSHIP WERE AT LEISURE, I SHOULD IMPART A THING TO YOU FROM HIS MAJESTY.

I WILL RECEIVE IT WITH ALL DILIGENCE OF SPIRIT.

I THANK YOUR LORDSHIP, 'TIS VERY HOT.
NO, BELIEVE ME, 'TIS VERY COLD; THE WIND IS NORTHERLY.
IT IS INDIFFERENT COLD, MY LORD, INDEED.

PUT YOUR BONNET TO HIS RIGHT USE; 'TIS FOR THE HEAD.

WHIP!
EXCEEDINGLY, MY LORD; IT IS VERY SULTRY - AS 'TWERE - I CANNOT TELL HOW.

BUT YET METHINKS IT IS VERY SULTRY AND HOT FOR MY COMPLEXION.

I BESEECH YOU, REMEMBER -

BUT, MY LORD, HIS MAJESTY BADE ME SIGNIFY TO YOU THAT HE HAS LAID A GREAT WAGER ON YOUR HEAD.
SIR, THIS IS THE MATTER -

NAY, GOOD MY LORD; FOR MINE EASE, IN GOOD FAITH.

SIR, HERE IS NEWLY COME TO COURT LAERTES; BELIEVE ME, AN ABSOLUTE GENTLEMAN, FULL OF MOST EXCELLENT DIFFERENCES, OF VERY SOFT SOCIETY AND GREAT SHOWING.
INDEED, TO SPEAK FEELINGLY OF HIM, HE IS THE CARD OR CALENDAR OF GENTRY, FOR YOU SHALL FIND IN HIM THE CONTINENT OF WHAT PART A GENTLEMAN WOULD SEE.
SIR, HIS DEFINEMENT SUFFERS NO PERDITION IN YOU, THOUGH, I KNOW, TO DIVIDE HIM INVENTORIALLY WOULD DIZZY THE ARITHMETIC OF MEMORY, AND YET BUT YAW NEITHER, IN RESPECT OF HIS QUICK SAIL.
BUT, IN THE VERITY OF EXTOLMENT, I TAKE HIM TO BE A SOUL OF GREAT ARTICLE AND HIS INFUSION OF SUCH DEARTH AND RARENESS, AS, TO MAKE TRUE DICTION OF HIM, HIS SEMBLABLE IS HIS MIRROR AND WHO ELSE WOULD TRACE HIM HIS UMBRAGE, NOTHING MORE.
YOUR LORDSHIP SPEAKS MOST INFALLIBLY OF HIM.
THE CONCERNANCY, SIR? WHY DO WE WRAP THE GENTLEMAN IN OUR MORE RAWER BREATH?
SIR?
IS'T NOT POSSIBLE TO UNDERSTAND IN ANOTHER TONGUE? YOU WILL DO'T, SIR, REALLY.

HIS PURSE IS EMPTY ALREADY; ALL'S GOLDEN WORDS ARE SPENT.

WHAT IMPORTS THE NOMINATION OF THIS GENTLEMAN?
OF LAERTES?

OF HIM, SIR.

YOU ARE NOT IGNORANT OF WHAT EXCELLENCE LAERTES IS -

I KNOW YOU ARE NOT IGNORANT -
I WOULD YOU DID, SIR; YET, IN FAITH, IF YOU DID, IT WOULD NOT MUCH APPROVE ME. WELL, SIR?
I DARE NOT CONFESS THAT, LEST I SHOULD COMPARE WITH HIM IN EXCELLENCE;
BUT TO KNOW A MAN WELL WERE TO KNOW HIMSELF.

WHAT'S HIS WEAPON?
I MEAN, SIR, FOR HIS WEAPON; BUT IN THE IMPUTATION LAID ON HIM BY THEM, IN HIS MEED HE'S UNFELLOWED.

THAT'S TWO OF HIS WEAPONS. BUT WELL.

RAPIER AND DAGGER.
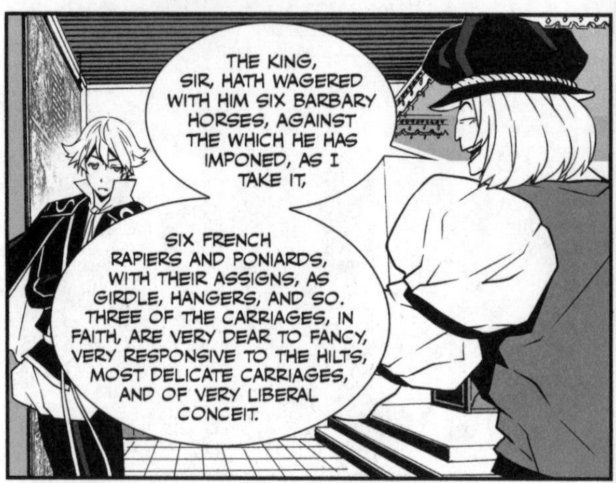
THE KING, SIR, HATH WAGERED WITH HIM SIX BARBARY HORSES, AGAINST THE WHICH HE HAS IMPONED, AS I TAKE IT,
SIX FRENCH RAPIERS AND PONIARDS, WITH THEIR ASSIGNS, AS GIRDLE, HANGERS, AND SO. THREE OF THE CARRIAGES, IN FAITH, ARE VERY DEAR TO FANCY, VERY RESPONSIVE TO THE HILTS, MOST DELICATE CARRIAGES, AND OF VERY LIBERAL CONCEIT.

WHAT CALL YOU THE CARRIAGES?
I KNEW YOU MUST BE EDIFIED BY THE MARGIN ERE YOU HAD DONE.
THE CARRIAGES, SIR, ARE THE HANGERS.
WHY IS THIS ALL IMPONED, AS YOU CALL IT?
THE PHRASE WOULD BE MORE GERMAN TO THE MATTER IF WE COULD CARRY CANNON BY OUR SIDES. I WOULD IT MIGHT BE HANGERS TILL THEN.
BUT, ON: SIX BARBARY HORSES AGAINST SIX FRENCH SWORDS, THEIR ASSIGNS, AND THREE LIBERAL-CONCEITED CARRIAGES:
THAT'S THE FRENCH BET AGAINST THE DANISH.
THE KING, SIR, HATH LAID THAT IN A DOZEN PASSES BETWEEN YOURSELF AND HIM, HE SHALL NOT EXCEED YOU THREE HITS.
HE HATH LAID ON TWELVE FOR NINE. AND IT WOULD COME TO IMMEDIATE TRIAL, IF YOUR LORDSHIP WOULD VOUCHSAFE THE ANSWER.

HOW IF
I ANSWER
'NO'?

I MEAN, MY LORD, THE OPPOSITION OF YOUR PERSON IN TRIAL.
FLAP

SIR, I WILL WALK HERE IN THE HALL.

IF IT PLEASE HIS MAJESTY, 'TIS THE BREATHING TIME OF DAY WITH ME.
LET THE FOILS BE BROUGHT, THE GENTLEMAN WILLING, AND THE KING HOLD HIS PURPOSE, I WILL WIN FOR HIM IF I CAN;
IF NOT, I WILL GAIN NOTHING BUT MY SHAME AND THE ODD HITS.

TO THIS EFFECT, SIR; AFTER WHAT FLOURISH YOUR NATURE WILL.
I COMMEND MY DUTY TO YOUR LORDSHIP.
SHALL I RE-DELIVER YOU E'EN SO?
ZOOM-
YOURS, YOURS.
HE DOES WELL TO COMMEND IT HIMSELF; THERE ARE NO TONGUES ELSE FOR'S TURN.
THIS LAPWING RUNS AWAY WITH THE SHELL ON HIS HEAD.
HE DID COMPLY WITH HIS DUG, BEFORE HE SUCKED IT.

ONLY GOT THE TUNE OF THE TIME AND OUTWARD HABIT OF ENCOUNTER;
THUS HAS HE - AND MANY MORE OF THE SAME BEVY THAT I KNOW THE DROSSY AGE DOTES ON -
A KIND OF YEASTY COLLECTION, WHICH CARRIES THEM THROUGH AND THROUGH THE MOST FOND AND WINNOWED OPINIONS;
AND DO BUT BLOW THEM TO THEIR TRIAL, THE BUBBLES ARE OUT.
MY LORD, HIS MAJESTY COMMENDED HIM TO YOU BY YOUNG OSRIC, WHO BRINGS BACK TO HIM THAT YOU ATTEND HIM IN THE HALL.
HE SENDS TO KNOW IF YOUR PLEASURE HOLD TO PLAY WITH LAERTES, OR THAT YOU WILL TAKE LONGER TIME.
I AM CONSTANT TO MY PURPOSES; THEY FOLLOW THE KING'S PLEASURE.
IF HIS FITNESS SPEAKS, MINE IS READY. NOW OR WHENSOEVER, PROVIDED I BE SO ABLE AS NOW.
THE KING AND QUEEN AND ALL ARE COMING DOWN.
IN HAPPY TIME.
THE QUEEN DESIRES YOU TO USE SOME GENTLE ENTERTAINMENT TO LAERTES BEFORE YOU FALL TO PLAY.

SHE WELL INSTRUCTS ME.

BOW~

YOU WILL LOSE THIS WAGER, MY LORD.

I DO NOT THINK SO. SINCE HE WENT INTO FRANCE, I HAVE BEEN IN CONTINUAL PRACTISE. I SHALL WIN AT THE ODDS. BUT THOU WOULDST NOT THINK HOW ILL ALL'S HERE ABOUT MY HEART: BUT IT IS NO MATTER.

NAY, GOOD MY LORD.

IT IS BUT FOOLERY; BUT IT IS SUCH A KIND OF GAIN-GIVING, AS WOULD PERHAPS TROUBLE A WOMAN.

IF YOUR MIND DISLIKE ANY THING, OBEY IT. I WILL FORESTALL THEIR REPAIR HITHER, AND SAY YOU ARE NOT FIT.
NOT A WHIT, WE DEFY AUGURY. THERE'S A SPECIAL PROVIDENCE IN THE FALL OF A SPARROW.
LET BE.
PAT PAT
BWA-BWAAA!
!
IF IT BE NOW, 'TIS NOT TO COME; IF IT BE NOT TO COME, IT WILL BE NOW;
IF IT BE NOT NOW, YET IT WILL COME. THE READINESS IS ALL.
SINCE NO MAN HAS AUGHT OF WHAT HE LEAVES, WHAT IS'T TO LEAVE BETIMES?

MURMUR–
MURMUR–
COME, HAMLET, COME, AND TAKE THIS HAND FROM ME.

GIVE ME YOUR PARDON, SIR. I'VE DONE YOU WRONG; BUT PARDON'T, AS YOU ARE A GENTLEMAN.

THIS PRESENCE KNOWS, AND YOU MUST NEEDS HAVE HEARD, HOW I AM PUNISH'D WITH SORE DISTRACTION.

WHAT I HAVE DONE, THAT MIGHT YOUR NATURE, HONOUR AND EXCEPTION ROUGHLY AWAKE, I HERE PROCLAIM WAS MADNESS.

CLASP

WAS'T HAMLET WRONG'D LAERTES? NEVER HAMLET.

I AM SATISFIED IN NATURE, WHOSE MOTIVE, IN THIS CASE, SHOULD STIR ME MOST TO MY REVENGE.

BUT IN MY TERMS OF HONOUR I STAND ALOOF, AND WILL NO RECONCILEMENT

TILL BY SOME ELDER MASTERS, OF KNOWN HONOUR, I HAVE A VOICE AND PRECEDENT OF PEACE TO KEEP MY NAME UNGORED.

IF HAMLET FROM HIMSELF BE TA'EN AWAY, AND WHEN HE'S NOT HIMSELF DOES WRONG LAERTES, THEN HAMLET DOES IT NOT, HAMLET DENIES IT. WHO DOES IT, THEN? HIS MADNESS.

IF'T BE SO, HAMLET IS OF THE FACTION THAT IS WRONG'D; HIS MADNESS IS POOR HAMLET'S ENEMY.

SIR, IN THIS AUDIENCE, LET MY DISCLAIMING FROM A PURPOSED EVIL FREE ME SO FAR IN YOUR MOST GENEROUS THOUGHTS THAT I HAVE SHOT MINE ARROW O'ER THE HOUSE AND HURT MY BROTHER.

BUT TILL THAT TIME, I DO RECEIVE YOUR OFFER'D LOVE LIKE LOVE, AND WILL NOT WRONG IT.
I EMBRACE IT FREELY, AND WILL THIS BROTHER'S WAGER FRANKLY PLAY.

COME, ONE FOR ME.
- GIVE US THE FOILS. COME ON.

YOU MOCK ME, SIR.

NO, BY THIS HAND.

I'LL BE YOUR FOIL, LAERTES;
IN MINE IGNORANCE YOUR SKILL SHALL, LIKE A STAR I' THE DARKEST NIGHT, STICK FIERY OFF INDEED.

GIVE THEM THE FOILS, YOUNG OSRIC.

VERY WELL, MY LORD. YOUR GRACE HATH LAID THE ODDS O' THE WEAKER SIDE.

COUSIN HAMLET, YOU KNOW THE WAGER?

I DO NOT FEAR IT. I HAVE SEEN YOU BOTH. BUT SINCE HE IS BETTER'D, WE HAVE THEREFORE ODDS.

THIS IS TOO HEAVY.

LET ME SEE ANOTHER.
CLICK
GRAB!
THIS LIKES ME WELL. THESE FOILS HAVE ALL A LENGTH?

VWIP!
VWIP!

AY, MY GOOD LORD.

IF HAMLET GIVE THE FIRST OR SECOND HIT, OR QUIT IN ANSWER OF THE THIRD EXCHANGE, LET ALL THE BATTLEMENTS THEIR ORDNANCE FIRE;

THE KING SHALL DRINK TO HAMLET'S BETTER BREATH, AND IN THE CUP AN UNION SHALL HE THROW RICHER THAN THAT WHICH FOUR SUCCESSIVE KINGS IN DENMARK'S CROWN HAVE WORN.

SET ME THE STOUPS OF WINE UPON THAT TABLE.

AND LET THE KETTLE TO THE TRUMPET SPEAK, THE TRUMPET TO THE CANNONEER WITHOUT, THE CANNONS TO THE HEAVENS, THE HEAVENS TO EARTH, 'NOW THE KING DRINKS TO HAMLET.'

GIVE ME THE CUPS;

COME, BEGIN.

GLUG...

COME ON, SIR.

COME, MY LORD.

NOD

AND YOU, THE JUDGES, BEAR A WARY EYE.

TANG
TANG
TANG
TANG
SHING
SHING
FWAP!
ONE.
JUDGMENT.
NO.

WELL; AGAIN.
RAGH!

A HIT, A VERY PALPABLE HIT.

HAMLET, THIS PEARL IS THINE; HERE'S TO THY HEALTH.

STAY, GIVE ME DRINK.

GIVE HIM THE CUP.

PLIP!

I'LL PLAY THIS BOUT FIRST; SET IT BY AWHILE.

COME.

...

KA-TNG
CLANG
TANG
CLANG
VWSSH!
KA-TANNNG
WHIP~

FWUD
ANOTHER HIT; WHAT SAY YOU?
A TOUCH, A TOUCH, I DO CONFESS.
NRRRGH..
HE'S FAT, AND SCANT OF BREATH.
OUR SON SHALL WIN.

HERE, HAMLET, TAKE MY NAPKIN, RUB THY BROWS. THE QUEEN CAROUSES TO THY FORTUNE, HAMLET.
GOOD MADAM!
SIP
I WILL, MY LORD; I PRAY YOU, PARDON ME.
GERTRUDE, DO NOT DRINK.

IT IS THE POISON'D CUP; IT IS TOO LATE.
I DARE NOT DRINK YET, MADAM. BY AND BY.
COME, LET ME WIPE THY FACE.

I DO NOT THINK'T.

MY LORD, I'LL HIT HIM NOW.

AND YET 'TIS ALMOST 'GAINST MY CONSCIENCE.
SHUF

COME, FOR THE THIRD, LAERTES. YOU DO BUT DALLY.
I PRAY YOU, PASS WITH YOUR BEST VIOLENCE. I AM AFEARD YOU MAKE A WANTON OF ME.

SAY YOU SO? COME ON.
CLANG
CLASH!
TANG
TING
NOTHING NEITHER WAY.
SHING!

HUFF
HUFF
TINK.
HUFF...
CLANG
SNATCH
BLUB
HAVE AT YOU NOW!

SLASH-
CRASH
CLANG
CLASH
WHSSH-
WHUD!
WHAM!

SLIP!
CLANG
WHIP!
CRASH
OH!
CLANG-
RAAGH
WHUD

WHOMPF

WHUMPA
CLANG!
WHUMPA
CLAT!

NNNGH...

!
WHUMP

RGH!
GRAB
WHUMP-
RRRAH!

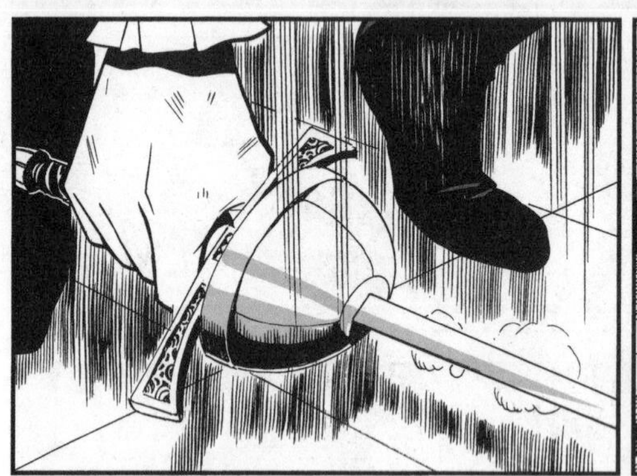

SHHHANG

RAAAAAAH-

WHUMP
CLASH
CLANG
TING

RAAAAGH
WHAM

PART THEM; THEY ARE INCENSED.

WHUD!
NAY, COME, AGAIN!

AAAAGHCK!
FLUMP
LOOK TO THE QUEEN THERE, HO!
SLA-ASH-!

GHHCK!
KA-HACK...
THEY BLEED ON BOTH SIDES.
WHUD
HOW IS'T, LAERTES?
HOW IS IT, MY LORD?
SHUDDER
WHY, AS A WOODCOCK TO MINE OWN SPRINGE, OSRIC.

KA-HACK

I AM JUSTLY KILL'D WITH MINE OWN TREACHERY.

NO, NO, THE DRINK, THE DRINK -

HOW DOES THE QUEEN?

SHE SWOONS TO SEE THEM BLEED.

FWUMP.
THE DRINK, THE DRINK! I AM POISON'D.

HO!
LET THE DOOR
BE LOCK'D:

TREACHERY! SEEK IT OUT.
IT IS HERE, HAMLET.
LO, HERE I LIE NEVER TO RISE AGAIN. THY MOTHER'S POISON'D.
HAMLET, THOU ART SLAIN. NO MEDICINE IN THE WORLD CAN DO THEE GOOD. IN THEE THERE IS NOT HALF AN HOUR OF LIFE;
THE TREACHEROUS INSTRUMENT IS IN THY HAND, UNBATED AND ENVENOM'D. THE FOUL PRACTICE HATH TURN'D ITSELF ON ME.
I CAN NO MORE. THE KING, THE KING'S TO BLAME.

THE POINT! - ENVENOM'D TOO!
THEN, VENOM, TO THY WORK.
WHAM!
DASH-

SLASH!
TREASON! TREASON!
O, YET DEFEND ME, FRIENDS. I AM BUT HURT.
HERE, THOU INCESTUOUS, MURDEROUS, DAMNED DANE, DRINK OFF THIS POTION. IS THY UNION HERE?

SPLASH!

FOLLOW MY MOTHER.

GACK-!

IT IS A POISON TEMPER'D BY HIMSELF.

HE IS JUSTLY SERVED.
EXCHANGE FORGIVENESS WITH ME, NOBLE HAMLET.

MINE AND MY FATHER'S DEATH COME NOT UPON THEE, NOR THINE ON ME.

HEAVEN MAKE THEE FREE OF IT! I FOLLOW THEE.
SHUDDER

I AM DEAD, HORATIO.

HORATIO, I AM DEAD; THOU LIVEST;
REPORT ME AND MY CAUSE ARIGHT TO THE UNSATISFIED.

WRETCHED QUEEN, ADIEU!
YOU THAT LOOK PALE AND TREMBLE AT THIS CHANCE, THAT ARE BUT MUTES OR AUDIENCE TO THIS ACT, HAD I BUT TIME -
AS THIS FELL SERGEANT, DEATH, IS STRICT IN HIS ARREST - O, I COULD TELL YOU - BUT LET IT BE.

NEVER BELIEVE IT. I AM MORE AN ANTIQUE ROMAN THAN A DANE. HERE'S YET SOME LIQUOR LEFT.

!!

AS THOU'RT A MAN, GIVE ME THE CUP.

LET GO; BY HEAVEN, I'LL HAVE'T.

WHAP!

CLANG!

NNG!

NNGH...

O GOOD HORATIO, WHAT A WOUNDED NAME, THINGS STANDING THUS UNKNOWN, SHALL LIVE BEHIND ME!
IF THOU DIDST EVER HOLD ME IN THY HEART ABSENT THEE FROM FELICITY AWHILE, AND IN THIS HARSH WORLD DRAW THY BREATH IN PAIN, TO TELL MY STORY.

KAAAGH!
BOOM!
BOOM!
YOUNG FORTINBRAS, WITH CONQUEST COME FROM POLAND, TO THE AMBASSADORS OF ENGLAND GIVES THIS WARLIKE VOLLEY.
WHAT WARLIKE NOISE IS THIS?
O, I DIE, HORATIO.
THE POTENT POISON QUITE O'ER-CROWS MY SPIRIT: I CANNOT LIVE TO HEAR THE NEWS FROM ENGLAND,
BUT I DO PROPHESY THE ELECTION LIGHTS ON FORTINBRAS. HE HAS MY DYING VOICE.

SO TELL HIM, WITH THE OCCURRENTS MORE AND LESS, WHICH HAVE SOLICITED.
THE REST IS SILENCE.
GA-HACK!
NOW CRACKS A NOBLE HEART. GOOD NIGHT, SWEET PRINCE, AND FLIGHTS OF ANGELS SING THEE TO THY REST!

CLANK
CLANK
CLANK
WHY DOES THE DRUM COME HITHER?
WHERE IS THIS SIGHT?
THIS QUARRY CRIES ON HAVOC.
O PROUD DEATH, WHAT FEAST IS TOWARD IN THINE ETERNAL CELL, THAT THOU SO MANY PRINCES AT A SHOT SO BLOODILY HAST STRUCK?
WHAT IS IT YE WOULD SEE? IF AUGHT OF WOE OR WONDER, CEASE YOUR SEARCH.
THE SIGHT IS DISMAL; AND OUR AFFAIRS FROM ENGLAND COME TOO LATE.

THE EARS ARE SENSELESS THAT SHOULD GIVE US HEARING, TO TELL HIM HIS COMMANDMENT IS FULFILL'D,

NOT FROM HIS MOUTH, HAD IT THE ABILITY OF LIFE TO THANK YOU. HE NEVER GAVE COMMANDMENT FOR THEIR DEATH. BUT SINCE, SO JUMP UPON THIS BLOODY QUESTION,

THAT ROSENCRANTZ AND GUILDENSTERN ARE DEAD. WHERE SHOULD WE HAVE OUR THANKS?

ARE HERE ARRIVED, GIVE ORDER THAT THESE BODIES HIGH ON A STAGE BE PLACED TO THE VIEW, AND LET ME SPEAK TO THE YET UNKNOWING WORLD HOW THESE THINGS CAME ABOUT.

AND YOU FROM ENGLAND

YOU FROM THE POLACK WARS,

SO SHALL YOU HEAR OF CARNAL, BLOODY, AND UNNATURAL ACTS, OF ACCIDENTAL JUDGMENTS, CASUAL SLAUGHTERS,

OF DEATHS PUT ON BY CUNNING AND FORCED CAUSE, AND, IN THIS UPSHOT, PURPOSES MISTOOK FALL'N ON THE INVENTORS' HEADS.

ALL THIS CAN I TRULY DELIVER.

FOR ME, WITH SORROW I EMBRACE MY FORTUNE.
I HAVE SOME RIGHTS OF MEMORY IN THIS KINGDOM, WHICH NOW TO CLAIM MY VANTAGE DOTH INVITE ME.
FWUMP

LET US HASTE TO HEAR IT, AND CALL THE NOBLEST TO THE AUDIENCE.

LET FOUR CAPTAINS BEAR HAMLET, LIKE A SOLDIER, TO THE STAGE; FOR HE WAS LIKELY, HAD HE BEEN PUT ON, TO HAVE PROVED MOST ROYALLY;

OF THAT I SHALL HAVE ALSO CAUSE TO SPEAK, AND FROM HIS MOUTH WHOSE VOICE WILL DRAW ON MORE.
BUT LET THIS SAME BE PRESENTLY PERFORM'D, EVEN WHILE MEN'S MINDS ARE WILD, LEST MORE MISCHANCE ON PLOTS AND ERRORS HAPPEN.

AND, FOR HIS PASSAGE, THE SOLDIERS' MUSIC AND THE RITES OF WAR SPEAK LOUDLY FOR HIM. TAKE UP THE BODIES. SUCH A SIGHT AS THIS BECOMES THE FIELD, BUT HERE SHOWS MUCH AMISS.
GO, BID THE SOLDIERS SHOOT.

BA-BA-BAM!

BAM!

BA-BAM! BAM!
BA-BA-BAM!

~ *FINALE* ~

I want to explain this design a little further: the Hamlet at the top, with his sword up and ready to charge, represents his desire to take vengeance. The Hamlet in the center, with his sword at his own throat, represents his desire to kill himself. And the skull at the bottom of the page represents Hamlet's musings on death. That's how we avoided leading the readers to a single explanation for the line, which would stop them from thinking about the others.

ADDING A CAST APPEARANCE:

Readers who are familiar with the play may be curious about Ophelia's appearance in *Act II, Scene 2*, since she does not appear there in the original scene. Actually, it's because at the end of *Act II, Scene 1*, Polonius tells Ophelia, "Come, go we to the King." Since he said that, it made sense for Ophelia to be by his side in the next scene. Not only does this not conflict with the original, it actually enhances the plot a bit! For example, when Polonius reads Hamlet's love letter out loud to the King and Queen - the letter is very explicit, and poor Ophelia is ashamed and embarrassed when her father reads the line about her 'excellent white bosom'. Polonius is neglecting to take his daughter's feelings into account, invading her privacy in front of two non-family members - he sees her only as one of his assets, and he doesn't think twice about abusing her privacy in order to win points with the King. This is a relatively bold change for the *Manga Classics* Shakespeare books, but it does still remain true to the principle of being faithful to the original! I hope you like this change.

THAT'S AN ILL PHRASE, A VILE PHRASE; 'BEAUTIFIED' IS A VILE PHRASE: BUT YOU SHALL HEAR. THUS:
'IN HER EXCELLENT WHITE BOSOM, THESE, ETC.'
OH NO...

Continues on Page 3...

CRYSTAL S. CHAN:
ADAPTING HAMLET

Hamlet **is the fourth of Shakespeare's plays that I have adapted for manga. If you've read any of the others, then you know about my approach for adapting the script for a play - this time, I want to focus on my experiences in adapting the unique features of *Hamlet.***

HANDLING THE CLASSIC LINE:

First of all, I want to talk about how we handled the situation surrounding the famous line, "*To be, or not to be, that is the question.*" This line is very well-known, but not everyone agrees on exactly what it means. Generally, there are three possible explanations: Hamlet may be talking about killing himself, about killing other people in revenge, or simply musing about the nature of death.

Readers can make a reasonable and convincing argument for any one of these explanations. However, if I picked only one explanation for the artist to draw, then I would have set the tone for the rest of the book to follow, and the other two explanations would have been wiped out. Therefore, I explained the meaning of the speech to the artist and asked him to design a layout that can represent all three meanings. Andy, our production director, thought that the first try did not succeed in interpreting all the layers of meaning. After we got input from other team members, we created what is now the final version!

<ORIGINAL PAGE>

<FINAL PAGE>

remember it. In *Act III, Scene 3*, Lord Polonius says to King Claudius, "And, as you said (and wisely was it said) 'tis meet that some more audience than a mother - since nature makes them partial - should o'erhear the speech, of vantage." He's crediting the King with wisely saying that, but the King didn't say that - Polonius did, in *Act III, Scene 1*! Polonius is giving the King credit for the idea in order to flatter him. I showed the prior scene during this one to help the readers understand the intentions behind this action. It helps people to understand that Polonius is a man who loves to flatter his superiors.

ECHOING FEELINGS WITH ACTIONS:

I also used facial expressions and character actions to show characters' natures and dispositions. In *Act I, Scene 3*, Polonius forbids Ophelia from dating Hamlet. Ophelia tries to explain that Hamlet is serious about her, but Polonius will not change his mind, and Ophelia is forced to obey her father's decision. Under these circumstances I believe she would not be happy, so after her line "I shall obey, my lord" I asked the artist to draw her with her head down, looking upset. Polonius, walking in front of her, doesn't notice this, which is another example of him neglecting his daughter's feelings.

Continues on Page 5...

...continued from Page 2

VISUAL EXPRESSION OF STORYTELLING:

In addition to making some bold changes, I also used my adaptation techniques to visualize the figurative language so common in Shakespeare's plays. *Hamlet* takes these figurative scenes to new lengths. In *Act II, Scene 2*, the First Player tells Hamlet a very long story about Pyrrhus - it took us six pages to properly show the action.

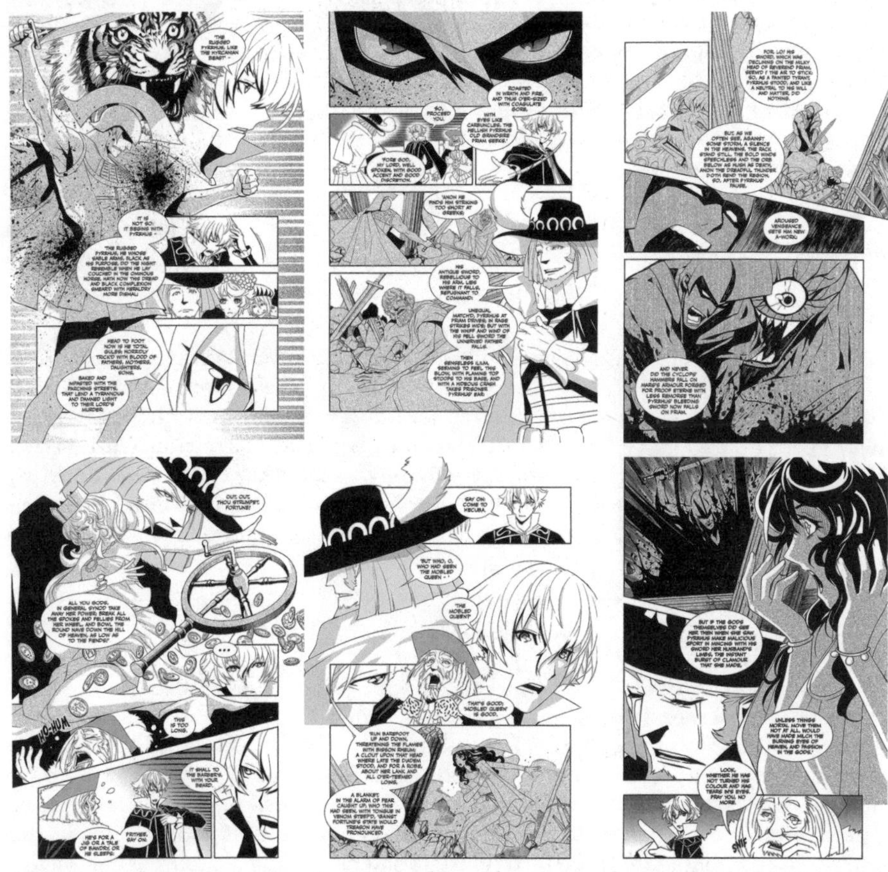

This shows how manga is a better medium than even the original play! Imagine how boring it would have been to watch the First Player talk forever without any addition visualization!

RECAPPING THE PLOT VISUALLY:

Since visualization is one of manga's strong points, I wanted to use it to my best advantage. For example, when a character recalls something that happened earlier in the story, I can 'flash back' and show that scene again, which helps the readers to

HANDLING THE "SPEECH":

One of Hamlet's characteristics is that he expresses his thoughts and emotions through monologue. First I studied lots of academic analysis of the monologue; then I thought about his changing mental state and made suggestions about actions that he might take in the script. For example, during his big speech in *Act II, Scene 2* - all the way from "Yet I, a dull and muddy-mettled rascal" to "the play's the thing wherein I'll catch the conscience of the king" - Hamlet goes from blaming himself for being too weak, to mocking his lack of bravery, to scolding the enemy who killed his father, to mocking himself for not taking vengeance yet, to demanding of himself that he rethink his plan, to finally planning his revenge, and finally being satisfied with his new plan. My notes on these actions helped the artist Julien understand the context faster and better, without having to stop and digest the content himself.

WORKING WITH THE ARTIST:

This is the fourth book I have worked on with Julien Choy. Based on our past experiences together, I knew how to arrange things in the script so that he could understand the story more easily. For example, in *Act II, Scene 2,* when Hamlet is pretending that he is crazy, I divided his dialogue into three 'types'. The first type of dialogue happens when Hamlet is alone and does not need to pretend he is crazy. The second type is when he has to pretend he is crazy in front of other people, but still needs to make sense. The third type is when he's saying something completely nonsensical in order to reinforce the idea that he's crazy. All three types of dialogue are included in this scene! I highlighted the lines in the script in different colors so that Julien could tell at a glance which Hamlet to draw.

Which leads me to another question: how do you draw a 'crazy' character and make them distinct? Julien, Tai, and I talked about this. After all, it's not something that happens every day in manga! Julien wasn't sure that it was enough to use actions and expressions. We considered various approaches and finally chose to use

Continues on Page 7...

...continued from Page 4

HINTS MADE BY THE PLOT:

Details can help the reader understand the story better. Look at *Act I, Scene 5*, when Horatio and Marcellus beg Hamlet to tell them about his meeting with his father's ghost. Hamlet says, "No, you'll reveal it." The artist, Julien, originally included only Horatio and Hamlet in this panel. Although that would have worked well enough, I asked him to include Marcellus and have Hamlet be looking at him instead. Why? Because later in the story, Hamlet trusts Horatio with that very secret! The reason he refused to tell them at that time was because he doubted Marcellus, not Horatio. It would have been misleading if we suggested that Hamlet didn't trust Horatio. This sort of thing isn't immediately obvious - however, by adding these details, we can make the story make more sense.

<ORIGINAL LAYOUT> **<FINAL PAGE>**

DRAWING DUPLICITY:

By using the strengths of manga wisely, good results can be achieved even without intentionally adding the details. It is much easier in manga to express the discrepancy between a character's actions and his true thoughts. For example, in Act II, Scene 2, Hamlet asks Rosencrantz and Guildenstern to stay nearby if they love him, saying, "If you love me, hold not off." In truth, he is actually thinking that he needs to keep them close in order to keep an eye on their actions, thinking, "Nay, then, I have an eye of you." By placing these two lines in the same panel, it becomes easy to show that what Hamlet is saying and what he is thinking are not the same thing at all.

trophy of war and can now be found in the National Museum in Stockholm. I was able to purchase some books about the arrases in the souvenir store, so I used those books to help us recreate the actual Kronborg of the time.

These two tapestries below were based on photos of the real thing - one of them we modified it to include young Hamlet and his father the King.

A FINAL FUN FACT:

One of the ferries that runs between Helsingør of Denmark and Helsingbord of Sweden is named 'Hamlet'. This isn't the first time I've seen such a thing - when I was researching locations for The Count of Monte Cristo, I rode on a ferry named 'Edmond Dantès'!

If a writer wants to create a version of a story with characters who are both appropriate to the time and easy for modern readers to understand, it is not enough to use only experiences from the past. I believe that this essay makes that very clear. The writer is required to think further than that, fitting the different parts of the play together and making the proper adjustments. Not only do I need to stay faithful to the original, I need to make the best of the play's features. I hope you enjoy my version of ***Hamlet***!

Crystal (Silvermoon) Chan

...continued from Page 6

famous paintings of Ophelia for reference: Julien drew both mad Hamlet and mad Ophelia with bare feet, suggesting that they were no longer sane enough to remember to wear shoes. However, that's not the only way to judge. If sane Hamlet and crazy Hamlet appear in the same scene, we can't exactly have him stop to put on his shoes when he's alone! The reader has to judge for themselves whether barefoot Hamlet is currently sane or not.

GIVING LINES CONTEXT THROUGH THE SETTING:

To research for this project, I visited the castle of Kronborg in Helsingør, Denmark, where Shakespeare originally set the play. Since I visited the place, I had to make good use of it as a setting for the manga! For example, in *Act IV, Scene 7*, I arranged for King Claudius and Laertes to have their murderous conversation in the basement of the castle, since the dark and remote location gave the whole thing a secretive air. That basement is a real location that you can visit in the castle! There is a statue of Ogier the Dane in it nowadays, which we have removed in our story, since that statue was installed in 1907 and was therefore of entirely the wrong time period.

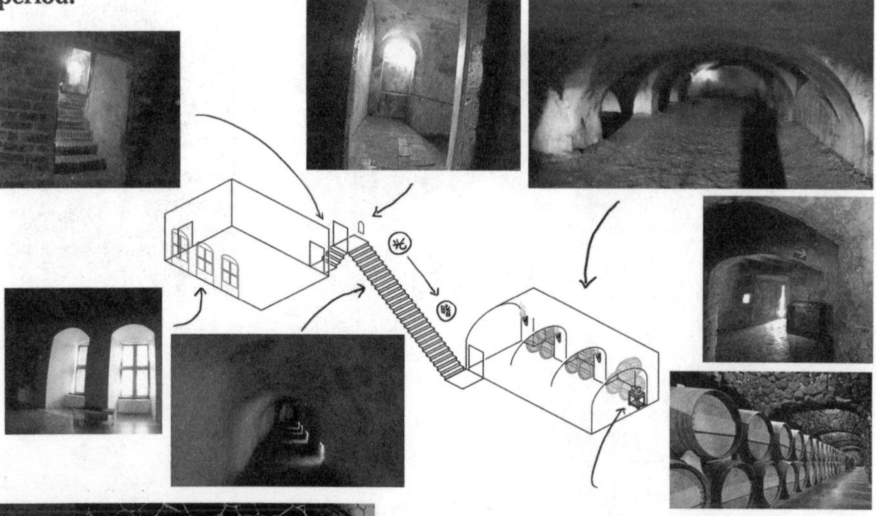

RECREATING THE SETS:

In *Act II, Scene 2*, Polonius wants to be 'behind an arras'. An arras is a tapestry, a common form of textile art found in Kronborg at the time of the play. Unfortunately, due to various reasons, some of the Kronborg arrases are no longer in their original locations. For example, the arras that Hamlet stabs Polonius through really exists - it was acquired by Sweden as a

KING HAMLET'S GHOST
QUEEN GERTRUDE
CLAUDIUS
LAERTES
POLONIUS
OPHELIA
HORATIO
ROSENCRANTZ
GUILDENSTERN

CHARACTER DESIGN SKETCHBOOK:
PRINCE HAMLET
hair design
facial expressions
costume design variations

This is the back of the book!

Manga Classics® books follow the Japanese comic (aka Manga!) reading order. Traditional manga is read in a "reversed" format starting on the right and heading towards the left. The story begins where English readers expect to find the last page because the spine of the book is on the opposite side. Flip to the other end of the book and start reading your Manga Classics!

WILLIAM SHAKESPEARE

Art by: Julien Choy

Story Adaptation by: Crystal S. Chan

Lettering: Daria Rhodes

STAFF:

Project Chief North America: Erik Ko
Editor: M. Chandler
VP of Sales: John Shableski
Production Manager: Janice Leung
Copy Editing: Michelle Lee

Project Chief Asia: Andy Hung
Production Manager: Yuen Him Tai
Art Assistants: Man Yiu
Peter Mak
Stoon

INTEREST LEVEL: 7-12 READING LEVEL: Grade 11 AGE: Young Adult (12+)

BISAC: YAF010060 YAF010010 YAF009000 YAF010000
CGN00600 DRA000000, FIC004000
Young Adult Fiction, Comics & Graphic Novels, Manga, Classic Adaptation

DEWEY 741.5

LIBRARY SUBJECT: Drama, Manga, Shakespeare, Classic Literature

Manga Classics: Hamlet. Published by Manga Classics, Inc. 118 Tower Hill Road, C1, PO Box 20008, Richmond Hill, Ontario, L4K 0K0, Canada. Any similarities to persons living or dead are purely coincidental. No portion of this publication may be used or reproduced by any means (digital or print) without written permission from Manga Classics Inc. except for review purposes. Manga Classics name is a registered trademark of Manga Classics, Inc. All artwork ©Manga Classics, Inc.

First Printing October 2019 Printed in Canada
HARD COVER EDITION ISBN # 978-1-947808-11-9 PAPERBACK EDITION ISBN # 978-1-947808-12-6

www.mangaclassics.com